Reframing the Early Childhood Curriculum

Research on young people's attitudes to the future highlights the extent to which they have difficulty coming to terms with it. They generally perceive it to be threateningly remote and uncertain, with recurring central themes including fear of the consequences of change, the threats of war, technical innovation and environmental destruction. Pre-school children, on the other hand, have a fundamentally different attitude towards the future and attendant notions of time and change. Early childhood professionals are thus optimally placed to lay important foundations for young children's long-term development.

Children maintain a positive and constructive outlook on life, have a strong sense of the continuity of time, are creative and imaginative and have a sense of personal connection with time and the future. All these qualities should be recognised and addressed in early childhood educational programmes as a means of counteracting the difficulty young people experience in knowing what to expect in their future lives and in coming to understand their roles in shaping them.

Reframing the Early Childhood Curriculum offers fresh insights by:

- examining futurists' and early childhood theorists' thinking of the relevance of planning for children's long-term needs in early childhood
- identifying the skills, attitudes and outlooks required to assist young children attending early childhood programmes in their long-term growth and development
- exploring the means through which these skills, attitudes and outlooks can be achieved in curriculum frameworks through specific goals and learning experiences against the background of young people's and young children's views of the future.

Jane M. Page is a lecturer in early childhood studies at the Department of Learning and Educational Development in the Faculty of Education at the University of Melbourne, Australia.

Futures and Education Series
General Editor: Richard A. Slaughter
Director of the Future Study Centre, Melbourne, Australia

New Thinking for a New Millennium
Richard A. Slaughter

Educating Beyond Violent Futures
Francis P. Hutchinson

Reframing the Early Childhood Curriculum
Educational Imperatives for the Future
Jane M. Page

Reframing the Early Childhood Curriculum

Educational Imperatives for the Future

Jane M. Page

London and New York

First published 2000
by RoutledgeFalmer
11 New Fetter Lane, London EC4P 4EE

RoutledgeFalmer is an imprint of the Taylor & Francis Group

© 2000 Jane M. Page

The right of Jane M. Page to be identified as the Author of this
Work has been asserted by her in accordance with the Copyright,
Designs and Patents Act 1988

Typeset in Times by Taylor & Francis Books Ltd
Printed and bound in Great Britain by Clays Ltd, St Ives plc

British Library Cataloguing in Publication Data
A catalogue record for this book is available from the British
Library

Library of Congress Cataloging in Publication Data
Page, Jane M., 1963–
Reframing the early childhood curriculum: educational imperatives
for the future/
Jane M. Page.
p. cm. – (Futures and education series)
Includes bibliographic references and index.
1. Early childhood education – Curriculum. 2. Education –
Forecasting.
I. Title. II. Series.
LB1139.4.P34 2000
372.19 – dc21

00-036625

ISBN 0–415–19117–3 (hbk)
ISBN 0–415–19118–1 (pbk)

For Christopher and Laura

Contents

Illustrations

Acknowledgements

This book has been facilitated by the assistance of many persons and organisations. It is with pleasure that I express my gratitude to them.

I am indebted to Professors Gillian Parmenter, Bridie Raban and Field Rickards for their support, interest and encouragement throughout the course of my Master of Education thesis 'Another World Like Here: Futures Studies and Early Childhood Education', and its subsequent revision and expansion into this book.

Professors Margaret Clyde and Richard Slaughter co-supervised my MEd. I owe Margaret Clyde a major debt of gratitude for providing me with unstinting advice, guidance, support and criticism. I am also greatly indebted to Richard Slaughter for his generous support, advice and sharing of information both in Australia and abroad.

Research outside Australia was made possible by grants from the Alice Creswick and Sheila Kimpton Foundation, the University of Melbourne, Faculty of Education Research Grant and a University of Melbourne Special Initiatives Grant.

My research outside Australia was greatly assisted by the counsel of individuals who generously shared their knowledge of the area with me. I am particularly indebted to Professoressa Eleanora Barbieri Masini, Università Pontifica Gregoriana, Rome, whose generosity and advice greatly assisted the research process in Italy. I would also like to note the assistance of Robert Jungk, Ray Lorenzo, World Wide Fund for Nature, Rome, Professoressa Augusta Busico, L'Età Verde, Rome, Barbara Goldfield, Economy Book and Video Centre, Rome, Peggy Ardwino, Olivia Sutton, Valerie Hughes, Core, the Co-operative School, Rome, Madame Anne-Marie Periera, Atelier des Enfants, Centre Georges Pompidou, Paris, Pierre Weiss, Unesco, Paris, Philippe de La Saussay, Centre de Prospective et d'Evaluation, Paris, Dirk Maxeiner, Munich, Dr David Hicks, Bath, Nicholas Albery, Institute for Social Inventions, London, Anne Parker, Barbican Art Gallery, London, Alison Manners, World Wide Fund for Nature, Education Department, London, Sharon Rodgers, Christopher Jones, Wendy Schultz, Social Science Research Institute, University of Hawai'i at Manoa, Honolulu, and Carol

Ann Brennan, University Elementary School, College of Education, Uni ver-sity of Hawaii, Honolulu. My studies were also assisted by the cooperation of staff at the Bibliotheca Hertziana, Rome, l'Association Internationale Futuribles, Paris, the Bernard Van Leer Foundation, the Hague, the Centre for Global Education, York, and the National Children's Bureau, London.

My research in Melbourne was greatly assisted by the generosity of Jan Deans and the staff, especially Angela, Kylie, Merryn and Sarah, children and families at the Children's Centre.

I would also like to thank my family, particularly my parents, friends and colleagues for their interest and encouragement. My final debt of gratitude is to Christopher for his unfailing support and to Laura for providing a further inspiration for this study.

Earlier versions of some of the material that appears in this volume has been published. An earlier version of chapter two was published as 'The Four- and Five-Year-Old's Understanding of the Future', in *Futures*, (1998), 30, 9: 913–22. An earlier version of chapter four appeared as 'Education Systems as Agents of Change: An Overview of Futures Education', in R.A. Slaughter (ed.) (1996) *New Thinking for a New Millennium*, London: Routledge. Sections of chapters five and six also appeared in a modified form as 'Futures in Early Childhood Education', in D. Hicks and R.A. Slaughter (eds) *World Yearbook of Education 1998: Futures Education*, London: Kogan Page.

Introduction

Well this is another world like here. Some builders heard it, someone told them that we should make another world, so they did.

(Charlotte, four years and ten months)

One of the most fundamental challenges facing educators is how to instil in children the attitudes, knowledge and outlooks they will require to function successfully as adults in the future. Their ability to respond to this imperative will depend, to a major degree, on the extent to which they can fashion systems and curricula that are truly responsive to the long-term developmental needs of the children in their care. Early childhood professionals have a particularly important role to play in this process. Positioned at the commencement of the education system, they are optimally placed to lay significant foundations for young children's lifelong development as they move towards adulthood and come to engage increasingly with a complex and often fragmented social environment.

The field of early childhood education has taken some steps towards achieving this goal by formulating curricula that are responsive to longer-term considerations. Recent studies have explored topics incorporating a futures orientation, such as environmental education, global education and peace studies. These issues, however, have been addressed in isolation and have lacked reference to an underlying methodology that might highlight their relative values and identify their shared concerns. Long-term developmental needs have also been commonly addressed through an emphasis on school readiness. For all its undeniable importance as a developmental consideration, this approach is nonetheless clearly inadequate as a broader framework assisting early childhood professionals to realise their potential to play a vital role in imparting the skills, attitudes and aspirations which are central to young children's development not just at school but also throughout their later lives.

This study aims to redress a significant imbalance in early childhood curriculum research. It will highlight the potential of the discipline of futures studies to assist early childhood practitioners in formulating curricula that are fully responsive to young children's longer-term considerations. Futures studies offers frameworks for understanding the challenges and potentials involved in the concepts of change and the future. It encourages individuals to counterbalance their instinctive fear of change with a recognition of the positive dimension of future time. It assists individuals to perceive the extent to which the future, far from being abstract and remote, is an immediately relevant and accessible principle of our lives. The relevance of these outlooks and skills becomes increasingly clear when examining the conclusions drawn in a growing body of global research on young people's attitudes to the future. This research consistently highlights the extent to which young people have difficulty coming to terms with the future, which they generally perceive to be threateningly remote and uncertain. These attitudes point to a vacuum of understanding about the future which educators should seek to fill with fully considered frameworks of understanding.

Futures studies has been applied widely in primary and secondary educational settings but has not, hitherto, been applied in the context of early childhood education. An examination of its principles and objectives highlights the degree to which it shares much in common with the pre-existing aims of early childhood education. The implementation of a futures-focused curriculum thus need not involve early childhood professionals in coming to terms with any radically new philosophical and educational frameworks. Rather, it provides educators with a means of extending and re-articulating existing developmental objectives from the vantage point of new perspectives.

The issue of whether futures concerns might be beyond the reach of four- and five-year-olds is central to any discussion concerning the formulation of a futures-based early childhood curriculum. Young children's attitudes towards the future and attendant notions of time and change differ fundamentally from those of adults. Yet their views should not be undervalued because they do not correspond to our own. They already possess many of the qualities stressed by adherents of futures studies as beneficial for a positive understanding of the future. Their flexibility of thought, their positive and constructive outlook on life, their sense of the continuity of time, their creativity and imagination, and their sense of personal connection with time and the future are all qualities which futures studies strives to re-instil in adults and older children. Their perspective on time and the future thus forms an ideal basis for a futures-focused curriculum.

Accordingly, an important first step towards formulating a futures-oriented early childhood curriculum should be for professionals to take seriously children's perceptions of the world. What is striking about the quotation that introduced this discussion, for example, is that Charlotte already perceives the future as being somehow distinct from the here and now of the present ('this is another world') and yet familiar and closely bound up with her experience ('like here'). This ability to combine a sense of

the abstract conceptual nature of the future with an emphasis on its immediate, personal relevance indicates that she already possesses one of the
central qualities of perception encouraged by futures education. By listening
to children, early childhood professionals will be in a better position to
formulate more responsive curricula that are grounded in the reality of
young children's understandings rather than guided by the ideals of an
educational framework formulated by others. This study seeks to assist early
childhood professionals towards realising this goal alongside the longer-
term considerations of children's growth and development.

Chapter 1

Children's rights and adults' responsibilities

Reinterpreting educational ethics

> There can be no task nobler than giving every child a better future.
> (World Declaration on the Survival, Protection and Development
> of Children, Unicef 1990: 165)

On 20 November 1989 the General Assembly of the United Nations unanimously endorsed the Convention on the Rights of the Child. Signed by a record sixty-one countries on the day of its opening for signature on 26 January 1990, it stood at the close of the century as one of the most widely ratified human rights treaties in the history of the United Nations. It remains at the onset of the millennium as a benchmark for global initiatives in the arena of children's rights. Among its key achievements is the recognition that it affords children, for the first time, that they should enjoy the same comprehensive range of civil, political, economic, social and cultural rights as are currently possessed by adults. It also strengthens its agenda with a call to state parties to assume a position of legal and moral responsibility and accountability in order to offer the administrative, legislative, judicial and other means necessary to advance the Convention's detailed and comprehensive charter for the future.

By enshrining these innovations at the highest level of global policy, the Convention constitutes an important documentary record of a paradigm shift in adults' attitudes towards children and their relationship to society. Earlier UN declarations and conventions had tended to address children's rights from a paternalistic perspective, viewing them primarily from the priorities of adults in their capacities as protectors and caregivers. The Convention, by contrast, recognises children as active agents of their own destinies. It sets out children's abilities and rights to form their own opinions and to participate actively in society and it seeks to safeguard children's rights to be heard in judicial and administrative proceedings which affect them. This emphasis on the rights of children to exercise autonomy in the decision-making process about factors influencing their lives has opened up a new and fundamentally important precedent in international law which is encapsulated in the key principle of the child's right to be heard.

The global prioritisation of children's rights further demonstrates a fundamental recognition of the importance of young children for long-term social growth and development. This emphasis was subsequently ratified and expanded on by initiatives set in train by the Convention, such as the World Summit for Children's Plan of Action for Implementing the World Declaration in the 1990s:

> As today's children are the citizens of tomorrow's world, their survival, protection and development is a prerequisite for the future development of humanity. Empowerment of the younger generation with knowledge and resources to meet their basic human needs and to grow to their full potential should be a primary goal of national development.
>
> (Unicef 1990: 166)

As a primary means of implementing these objectives, the Convention stresses the importance of education in fostering children's broader outlooks and attitudes for the future. It accordingly calls on educational curricula to foster:

> the development of respect for human rights and fundamental freedoms ... for the child's parents, his or her own cultural identity, language and values, for the national values of the country in which the child is living, the country from which he or she may originate, and for civilisations different from his or her own ... [and] for the natural environment.

Viewed from this perspective, educators are seen as performing a fundamental role in helping to prepare children 'for responsible life in a free society, in the spirit of understanding, peace, tolerance, equality of sexes and friendship among all peoples, ethnic, national, religious groups and persons of indigenous origin' (Article 29).

The right to be heard: youth commentaries on the future

A first step in converting the globally oriented recommendations of the Convention to the more grounded requirements of tailored educational curricula might be to consider the fundamental premise outlined in the Convention that the child has a right to be heard. Young people are living the issues that educators are seeking to plan for in their curriculum frameworks. They have a keen sense of the wider forces that influence their lives and the impact of these issues on their growth and development. By listening to their voices we can gain fresh insights into how best to build the appropriate knowledge base and skills to assist them to negotiate the challenges they come across in the future, and to tailor a curriculum with added meaning for children as it responds to the reality of their life experiences.

The preoccupations and concerns identified in a growing body of international research on youth attitudes to the future strongly underline the need for a futures orientation in education. This research has highlighted consistently the degree to which young people have difficulty coming to terms with the future, which they generally view with trepidation and ambivalence: 'Recent surveys reveal a people who, beneath a professed personal optimism, nonchalance and hedonism, are fearful, pessimistic, bewildered, cynical and insecure; a people who feel destabilised and powerless in the face of accelerating cultural, economic and technological change' (Eckersley 1992: 10).

Central themes to emerge from these studies include young people's fear of the consequences of change, the threats of war, technological innovation and environmental destruction, themes which have remained central to young people's concerns from the 1980s through to the 1990s. The children surveyed by an American 1985 nationwide poll on the future, for example, expressed a bleak vision of a volatile world future (Wagschal and Johnson 1986: 666–9). Noel Wilson's summary of his 1983–4 Peace Dossier 13 project, in which he interviewed 600 Australian and British students aged fourteen to sixteen, contained a similar conclusion: 'Most of the young people believed there would be a nuclear war within their lifetime and that most people would die as a result of that war. Only six percent believed all human life would not be exterminated' (Wilson 1989: 37–8).

Equally negative attitudes towards the future were registered as far back as 1983 in interviews of Australian young people aged between ten and twelve. Characteristic of the study was one child's comment that:

> The world will be a wreck – there will be dead creatures everywhere, and the USA will be blown off the face of the earth. Mankind will be blowing up each other with deadly gases and all sorts of bombs. There will be creatures from other planets invading and no-one will survive. Everyone who thinks there will be flowers and birds are wrong, there will be destruction, death and diseases, and everyone will die painfully.
> (Anonymous interviewee, cited in Eckersley 1988a: attachment 1: 3)

More recently, researchers undertaking a 1991 study of eleven-year-olds living in Sydney were dismayed by the intensity of their subjects' feelings: 'nothing prepared us for the depth of the children's fear of the future, their despair about the state of our planet and their bleak predictions for their own nation' (*Sydney Morning Herald* researchers, cited in Eckersley 1992: 12). Several years later, Francis Hutchinson was struck by the same kinds of recurring response: 'I see the world in total disharmony and unease. So-called efforts to save the environment, to stop war, to erase poverty have been unsuccessful and failures. It's a world of total conflict' (Chris, cited in Hutchinson 1996: 80).

The manifestations of change

Perhaps the most fundamental factor contributing to the negativity registered in the research is a fear of the consequences of change. Those
interviewed in a survey on Australian community attitudes towards social
issues carried out in the 1980s expressed strong concern for the extent to
which Australian society seemed to be characterised by an increasingly rapid
rate of change. This uncertainty made it difficult for those interviewed to
feel that they were able to exert an influence over the forces shaping their
lives (V. Arbes, 'Present Tense: The Plight of Australians Today', Clemenger
Report, 1988, cited in Eckersley 1988a: 38). The 'Australian Values Survey'
of 1983 reached a similar conclusion with its finding that 60 per cent of
those interviewed were of the opinion that Australia was changing too
rapidly and that the uncertainty which this caused for the future meant that
it was best to live for the present (Roy Morgan Research Centre, 'Australian
Values Survey', 1986, cited in Eckersley: 1988a: 9).

The traumatic and unsettling manifestations of change created by the
threat of war appear throughout the research as a recurrent theme. The children interviewed by Wilson believed that war was inevitable and could not
be averted by the efforts of individuals. These findings were amplified by
subsequent studies by Tepperman, Curtis and Hutchinson. War was created
primarily by technology, which humans were powerless to control (Wilson
1989: 38; Tepperman and Curtis 1995: 553). 'The most prominent view I see
[of the twenty-first century] is that somewhere in the "centre" is a huge
atomic bomb in a glass shell. It is there to remind us that one day there will
be no future' (Clara, cited in Hutchinson 1996: 78).

The same fear of the inevitability of a technologically driven war was
expressed by those interviewed for the 1981 Mackay Report on technology
and the future (H. Mackay, 'Computers, Technology and the Future',
Mackay Report, cited in Eckersley 1988a: 16). Other Australian studies of
the 1980s gave equal emphasis to the threat of nuclear war (Eckersley 1988a:
25–7; Frydenberg and Lewis 1996: 275). Similar concerns were registered in
research undertaken in Canada, Finland, the USSR and Britain (Hicks
1988: 3). A 1987 national survey of ten- to seventeen-year-olds, undertaken
by the *Guardian*, found that the threat of war and nuclear weapons ranked
alongside unemployment, crime and violence as one of the foremost challenges facing the world (Hicks 1988: 3). Frances Hutchinson's research has
more recently highlighted that a significant proportion of young people
believe that war remains 'an intractable or unmalleable part of the future'
(Hutchinson 1996: 74).

Concerns over the greenhouse effect and the threat of global environmental destruction are also recurrent throughout the research (Frydenberg
and Lewis 1996: 275; Hutchinson 1996: 79). The children researched by
Hutchinson identified the destruction of the environment as their major

concern. Characteristic comments include: 'I see the environment in the future as a false representation of the real thing ... Forests that have been knocked down are made into forests of fibreglass and cement' (Anthony, cited in Hutchinson 1996: 79). Another similar one was:

> I saw a dry and dead environment ... the beaches and the air were destroyed by pollution and people were dying fast ... There were guns and fighting going on all over the world. Most people were poverty stricken and were forced to live in the streets ... The world to me wouldn't be worth living in.
>
> (Craig, cited in Hutchinson 1996: 79)

Many of the young people's responses combined fears about war and the environment with a broader fear of a pronounced ambivalence towards technological change and innovation. The Mackay Report, for example, posited a direct link between fear of the future and misgivings about technological change. Those interviewed commonly expressed the view that technology diminished the worth of the individual's contribution to society and widened the gap between rich and poor (H. Mackay 'Computers, Technology and the Future', the Mackay Report, cited in Eckersley 1988a: 16). Frances Hutchinson's study highlighted a similar loss of faith in human agency and a concern for 'a humanly and spiritually diminished world and a belief that the future will become more deeply divided between the haves and the have nots' (Hutchinson 1996: 77–8). This builds on findings published in a study on Australian attitudes towards science, technology and the future undertaken in 1987 by the Commission for the Future. While those interviewed welcomed technological progress, they also expressed a sense of powerlessness at their inability to control technological advances (MacGregor 1989: 32). Wilson's Peace Dossier 13 study of 1985 highlighted similar attitudes of fear, anger and hopelessness towards the inevitability of technological, social and political change (Wilson 1989: 36–9). The young people interviewed by a 1986 Australian Office of Youth Affairs Survey similarly identified technology as one of the most important contributors to unemployment (Eckersley 1988a: 27).

Global versus personal futures

It would certainly not be true to posit on the basis of the prevailing negative comments cited above a corresponding inability on young people's part to project their own identities into the future. In fact the children interviewed were often able to describe at great length what they felt their personal futures to be. They generally outlined these in much more positive terms than those provided for their visions of the global future. This disparity has been noted by a number of researchers (Wagschal and Johnson 1986: 666–7;

Eckersley 1988a: 9; MacGregor 1989: 31; H. Mackay, 'Computers, Technology and the Future', Mackay Report, cited in Eckersley 1992: 11). It points towards a gap between two poles of understanding which suggests an inability on the young people's part to perceive the connection which exists between their own personal futures and the global future dimension. The children understand that the global future will have some bearing on their lives, but they cannot comprehend how they are to exert an influence on shaping this future horizon. A corresponding sense of powerlessness is evident in many of their comments: 'I think of how a child would feel in this situation – scared, alone, frightened' (Caroline, cited in Hutchinson 1996: 75). Since these children cannot understand how they are to exert an influence on the future, they remain outside the picture of the global future, which remains both somehow relevant and yet abstract and alien at the same time. 'It is as though they believed that everything happening outside one's life simply by-passes the individual' (Toffler 1974: 11).

This sense of disconnection from the future highlights more general difficulties involved with understanding the concepts of change and the future themselves. The future is a complex and multidimensional concept which can be perceived from numerous differing viewpoints. It is, on the one hand, a vital and directly accessible governing principle of life. One indication of its immediacy in our lives is its direct influence on all our decisions in the present. Individuals form their decisions on the basis of projections of the result of their decisions, or of their hopes, fears and aspirations for the future. The future is, in this respect, directly continuous with the present and the past. It is not a separate or abstract zone whose influence upon the individual is to be regarded as remote and indeterminate. It is, rather, a force whose presence is felt every day of our lives, influencing all our actions and decisions in a most direct and immediate way. Its relevance and significance also lies in the manner in which it brings the actuality of the present and past into contact with the dynamism of what might be. The future connects individuals with their dreams and aspirations, offering them a field of potentiality where alternatives can be explored and new interpretative frameworks fashioned.

When regarded from this perspective, the future can or, indeed, should, as will be argued in this study, have the potential to empower individuals and to assist them to feel connected to the outside world of culture, society and the environment. But it would be overly idealistic, as we have seen, to define the future in such exclusively positive terms. As the research indicates, the future is more commonly perceived from the opposite viewpoint as a frighteningly unstable and unknowable force. This occurs partly as a result of the natural challenges presented by the concept of the future. The future can appear threatening, for example, because of its close association with the principle of change. There can be no doubt that, for all of us, the process of planning for and learning to adapt to change is often a challenging and threatening task since it forces us to move beyond the well-worn groove of routine and convention.

It is also possible to lose one's bearings in the concept of the future. The abstract nature of time, in particular, can encourage a sense of the future's inaccessibility. The time of five years in the past can be experienced relatively easily (notwithstanding the fact that no two individuals have experienced it in the same way) but it is more difficult to gain possession of the time of five years ahead. The conventional reference points for time, such as the calendar, hold less meaning in the future than they do for the present and past. This is because the limitlessness of future time has not yet been as systematically cultivated by the concrete reference points of experience. The future contains more areas of terra incognita than the past and present. This is why it needs so frequently to be described by analogy: a horizon with a continuously shifting perspective, for example, or a line or map. These analogies constitute useful conceptual tools which can assist individuals to give form to their understandings of the future. But they do not allow definitive possession of the future. It is beyond the power of individuals to possess the future in the same way that they are sometimes encouraged, albeit mistakenly, to believe that they can gain absolute possession of the present and past.

Disconnection and the engendering of cultural stereotypes

The research cited above bears vivid testimony to the extent to which individuals greatly fear that which they cannot control, that which impacts upon them but over which they have no sway. The fear of dying from a nuclear apocalypse or from a global environmental disaster, or of being made redundant by technological change, represents an expression of anxiety over a sense of disconnectedness from the future. This sense of disconnection noted above is evident in every level of the previously cited interviews. It is evident as much in the imagery drawn on by those interviewed as it is in the messages of alienation relayed to the interviewers. Recurrent within the interviews are images of increasing automation, computers, robots, nuclear weaponry and scientists taking over the future:

> There will be many computers and metallic space rockets. Pollution will be a big problem and food will be artificial. The population will decrease because of the poisoning air they will breath [sic]. There will be WARS which will kill and destroy. There will be water shortage and the sea will be poisoned. Transport will be big because they will manufacture hi-speed [sic] trains and motor buses. I don't the [sic] you will be able to know if it is day or night because you won't be able to see the sky.
>
> (Anonymous interviewee, cited in Eckersley 1988a: attachment 1: 2)

I saw a science and technology based planet where robots and machines are taking over. Life will be all mechanical ... that is, computer operated machines will dominate ... The environment will be mainly demolished and many animals will be extinct ... Wars will be very common ... What I saw seemed to me like one of those science-fiction movies.

(Mohamed cited in Hutchinson 1996: 78)

I fear the world in the twenty-first century will be much like a comic book science fiction story. Especially one like 'Judge Dredd' will become reality. If we don't attempt to bring these thoughts to the surface now, then the Earth will become a vast waste dump.

(Christopher cited in Hutchinson 1996: 80)

These negative descriptions draw closely and repeatedly on convention-alised, often stereotypical, science fiction imagery of the future. The young people interviewed have directly based their frameworks for analysis on the negative visions of the future which are so commonly encountered in science fiction film and literature. Films like *Terminator*, *Robo-Cop*, *Total Recall*, *Strange Days* and countless others project a vision of a terminally alienated and dehumanised future which has been ravaged by the effects of environmental and technological destruction. The imagery commonly encountered in these sources is identifiable as dystopian, or anti-Utopian, in its under-standing of the future (Clarke 1979: 225–51; Ross 1991: 137–67, 140–5). By accepting the conventions of this imagery, the young people further register their sense of disconnection from the global future. Their image of the global future represents an alien world which has been formed for them by conventionalised cultural values. By focusing on the fantastic and technolog-ical aspects of the future, they leave themselves out of the equation of what the future will be like (Wagschal and Johnson 1986: 668).

Imagery and the power of the media

We can better appreciate the ways in which such dystopian imagery is constructed if we consider briefly the role of the mass media in forming atti-tudes towards technology and the future. Television, the Internet and other modes of communication are critically important in this process since, besides family and peers, young people mainly engage with issues of the future through the mass media.

The mass media are not always as anti-educational as they are frequently depicted by their detractors. It is, nonetheless, true that the media are often non-critical in the sense that they are formatted for quick and easy consumption rather than for a prolonged exploration and discussion of issues. They also commonly encourage a predominantly passive exploration of issues which could be seen to encourage the feelings of alienation from the future outlined above (Wilson 1989: 37).

Advertising forms one of the major means by which values and attitudes are moulded for popular consumption. In advertisements, technology is frequently commodified as the ultimate object of desire. One particularly clear example of this tendency is a recent advertisement depicting a sleek, red sports-car which was accompanied by the simple caption, 'Sell the Kids'. The caption rendered apparent the motivation behind nearly all advertisements of this kind. Technology is no longer to be valued as a tool which is developed in order to enhance the spiritual and emotional well-being of humans in social relationships. It has become an absolute value in itself. The consumer's fundamental desire is now to acquire mastery of technology and its attendant values of power, prestige and success rather than to understand it as a means of enhancing social well-being. Idealised objects of desire generate a high degree of anxiety since the reality can never match the ideal. It is little wonder, therefore, that we noted previously the common perception of technology as a threatening, external force playing upon people's destinies.

An anxiety about technology is more clearly evident in the many images which emphasise the negative, dehumanising aspects of technology in the future. An illustration by the contemporary British illustrator Chris Foss connects an image of the future with a negative perception of technology in a manner which is characteristic of much post-war science fiction writing and illustration. The scene is set in a desolate, seemingly uninhabitable landscape which is dominated by the figure of a giant robot towering over and menacing the tiny human figures around it. The robot has assumed a human form, to the extent that a giant phallic space craft is seen to eject from between its legs. The conception of technology here presented follows a directly analogous process to that noted in the context of the advertisement and the children's statements on the future. Technology has been emphasised as an end in itself and has subsumed the human characteristics and attributes which it is ostensibly developed in order to support. The robot's anthropomorphism only serves further to emphasise its lack of humanity. The resulting impression of ironic alienation is directly comparable to the sentiments expressed in the previously discussed interviews.

Such is the strength of this negative stereotype of an alienated, technologically corrupted future, that its influence can be detected even in those images which have been formulated in order to help reverse its effects. An example of this is an advertisement circulated by the World Awareness Foundation regarding the destruction of natural resources by human rapacity. The advertisement takes the form of a ravenous monster menacing the world, which is composed of people's faces. A brief commentary exhorting the reader to act on the issue accompanies the image. It begins on a negative note by emphasising the extent to which human thoughtlessness is destroying the planet. A slightly more positive conclusion is reached with the statement that individuals should act on the matter 'before we lose it all', the implication being that if they act now the earth can still be saved. This suggestion, however, is undermined by the image itself which works against a positive message by focusing solely on the destruction evoked in the first stage of the commentary. That the advertisement disempowers the reader from acting is further underlined by the mass of merged faces, once again emphasising the effect of alienation and negating any sense of personal identification with the dilemma. The advertisement thus subverts its own agenda since there is no point in the reader doing anything when there is nothing in the advertisement to suggest that such an effort would be successful.

Additional factors influencing the development of negative attitudes towards the future

A number of other factors can be seen to have influenced young people's understandings of the future. Those from under-privileged backgrounds interviewed by Hutchinson commonly expressed a despairing and often violent vision of the future which formed a particularly negative group within the consistently negative attitudes towards the future expressed across social levels (Hutchinson 1996: 73, 75, 77, 80). The study also highlighted the extent to which children, even while drawing on cultural stereotypes of the future, tended to express them in ways which were relevant to their own background. This is exemplified by the statement of one individual from an under-privileged, urban environment that:

> There will be more street fighting, more colour gangs, bigger gangs, more street deaths. Life will be three times or more dangerous than now … Hoping that it won't happen but it will … People – such as pollies, big nobs – live in rose-coloured worlds and won't change. They won't take notice of kids.
>
> (Ann, cited in Hutchinson 1996: 75)

Gender also exerts an influence on the ways in which children see the future. Hutchinson has noted that young women have a greater concern for psychological violence in the future than their male counterparts who are more commonly preoccupied with the effects of war (Hutchinson 1996: 74). Frydenberg and Lewis found a greater concern for environmental issues and war amongst young women (Frydenberg and Lewis 1996: 277). The age of the interviewees has also been cited as a formative factor on their perceptions of the future. Digby, Boniecki, Davies and Eckersley all posit that fear of the future increases as children grow older (Digby 1983; G. Boniecki, unpublished manuscript, Centre for Environmental Studies, Macquarie

University *c*. early 1980s, cited in Eckersley 1988a: 11 and 18; R. Davies 'Children and the Threat of Nuclear War', 1987, cited in Hicks 1988: 4). Wilson goes so far as to state that a sense of the world being out of control begins as early as ten years of age and develops into a sense of fatalism by adolescence (Wilson 1989: 38).

Such conclusions take as their basis the wide body of research which emphasises the degree to which fear is a developmental factor. One such study, undertaken in 1987, concluded that fear becomes an appreciable factor in the attitudes of children aged eight and nine, and that it has significantly increased by the time children reach adolescence (R. Davies 'Children and the Threat of Nuclear War', cited in Hicks 1988: 4). Andrew Bennett's study contains the similar conclusion that types of fears increase in children as they grow older. Fears in early childhood will range from fear of loud noises, to fear of the unexpected and strangers, and separation anxiety. They develop at the ages of six to eight into fear of bodily harm, pain, robbers, kidnappers, violence and animals to fear of the supernatural and the mythical. In later childhood fears turn towards more realistic concerns such as sexuality, peer status and world-related events such as death, world destruction and nuclear devastation. By adolescence a correlation has been established between fear and the ability of adolescents to recognise their responsibility towards their futures and the environment (Bennett *et al.* 1992: 70–5).

Erika Landau's study of children's attitudes to the future similarly concludes that whereas children aged nine to twelve often ask generalised questions about the future which are not personally relevant, adolescents are more prepared to link understandings of the future with their own place in the world. With this advanced understanding of their relationship to the future comes a correspondingly greater sense of anxiety about the negative aspects of the future (Landau 1976: 155–6, 159). Both studies correlate with the earlier analyses of Erikson and Kohlberg, who recognised the link between adolescent developmental status and issues pertaining to the future. Hicks' and Holden's study with 400 children in the south-west of England, also found that optimism about personal and global futures decreased with age (Hicks and Holden 1995: 9).

Conclusions to be drawn from the research

A number of qualifications and areas for further consideration need to be taken into account when considering the research discussed above. There is, for example, the finding that young people draw on cultural stereotypes on the one hand, and the observation that these stereotypes are sometimes selectively chosen for their relevance to the social and economic situation of the individual on the other. There is also the issue of the influence of age on the responses of those interviewed. Finally, there is the question of whether the young people interviewed took their projections of the future entirely seriously or whether, as more recent commentators have begun to suggest, they might have recognised and played to a certain degree on the stereotypical nature of their comments, possibly as a means of articulating images of the future which they wished to avoid (Gough 1987a: 97, 1988a: 6–10; Eckersley 1988c: 37, 1997: 243–4). For all this uncertainty, there can be no doubt that the research surveyed here presents clear challenges to the educational system. The future is, to a significant extent, a matter of perception. It is a complex and, at times, challenging concept which often requires some work on the individual's part before he or she can overcome the negative interpretations that can attach themselves to it.

The research also highlights the importance of taking into account the developmental status of children when addressing their attitudes towards the future. We should, for example, expect adolescents to fear the future the most, since they are positioned at a particularly difficult developmental phase which represents an often uneasy transition from dependence to independence and which is often characterised by low self-esteem and a search for belonging and meaning (Eckersley 1988c: 37). It is during this period that children on their way to adulthood are required to come to terms with social institutions such as school or the workplace, which often heightens their awareness of the difficulties involved in the process of assimilating into society. Pre-school children, on the other hand, are important subjects for discussions of the future since they have not yet reached this complex developmental stage of ambivalence towards the outside world, as we shall see. Early childhood professionals should build on these attitudes in order to combat the problems experienced in adolescence.

A final and fundamental conclusion to be drawn from the research involves young people's lack of understanding of the future. That young people draw so commonly on dystopian visions of technology and the future establishes the pervasiveness of culturally generated stereotypes. Such stereotypes fill a vacuum of understanding about the future, a vacuum made all the more apparent by the previously noted disparity between young people's perceptions of personal and global futures. This lacuna of understanding provides fertile ground for the development of the misgivings and ambivalences so vividly expressed in the research discussed above. What is needed, therefore, is an alternative framework for understanding the future and an alternative forum in which to develop it. Educators need to assume leadership in offering these frameworks for understanding.

Chapter 2

Four- and five-year-old children's understandings of time and the future

The previous chapter drew on a growing body of research to explore the issue of youth commentaries on the future. Very little research exists, however, to guide our thinking on the fundamental issue of pre-school children's thinking about these issues. The handful of studies that are available have argued that young children tend to view the future much more positively than do older children. Ray Lorenzo, for example, cites an American comparison of the drawings of pre-school, primary and high school children which concluded that the pre-school children perceived the future in more positive and humorous terms than their older counterparts whose drawings depicted the future with a 'progressive lack of expressiveness and excitement' (Lorenzo 1989). Gisele Trommsdorff reached similar conclusions with the finding that children in first grade evaluated the future less positively than younger children and that their powers of anticipation were less developed than those of younger children (Trommsdorff 1993: 381–406). These findings correlate, in turn, with Hicks' related study of seven-year-old children and their older counterparts, which found that optimism towards personal and global futures decreases with age (Hicks 1996a: 1–13).

Young children's understanding of time

A major factor contributing to the imbalance in the literature on younger children's understanding of the future is the common perception that pre-school children have a limited sense of temporality. This is, of course, undeniably true in certain fundamental respects. Yet it should not detract from a recognition of the importance of young children's perceptions of the future. There can be no doubting that four- and five-year-old children's understandings of time differ significantly from the perception of time encountered in later years. Time, as it is understood in the adult sense, is a complex and abstract concept. As Piaget and others have underlined, the initial manifestations of the 'adult' understanding of time are only to be located from the age of about eight. At this point children can generally combine the ability to represent mental images of different moments and translate them into a chronology of time with an increasingly fluent acquisition and use of language (Piaget 1955; Whitrow 1980: 68–71). It is only at adolescence that children are able to understand fully the extent to which time is a coordinated, conventionalised framework for distinguishing temporal sequences which affects all objects equally and simultaneously.

There has been some debate concerning the validity of Piaget's developmental categories (Fleer 1992: 134–59). There is no essential disagreement, however, regarding his fundamental conclusion that a developing awareness of time is limited, from an adult point of view, by its being viewed in terms of the child's own activities. At the ages of four and five, time remains closely bound up in the child's actions and awareness. This understanding builds, in turn, on the younger child's earlier developmental stages which expressed a nascent understanding of time through tangibly concrete and direct, subjectively based terms. An example of this principle in operation is the manner in which babies learn to anticipate and overcome spatial and temporal distance by crying. Their attempts to bridge the gap of space and time with a call for gratification signals their fundamentally different understanding of time.

Piaget characterises the next stage of child development as one which manifests a developing understanding of duration and the distinctions between different states in a progression of events. Children will continue to frame these concepts in personally relevant terms during their subsequent development. At this point external events begin to appear as measurements for a developing sense of 'before' and 'after'. Extrinsic events are once again understood primarily in relation to the child's interactions with the environment (Piaget 1955: 325, 327, 344). Ego-centrism still remains evident, to a significant degree, in children aged four and five. When communicating with children of this age, the adult is required to translate the concept of the future into terms which are directly relevant to the routine of the children's experiences. Adults referring to an event which will occur in four days, thus need to explain that it will occur 'in four sleeps time'. The children with whom adults are communicating do not understand the concept of distance in time in an adult sense because they still do not recognise that time can ever be fully separate from them. The adult must thus express time in terms which emphasise its direct connection with them, even on a physical level.

It would be misleading to conclude from this that the young child's understanding is so under-developed as to disallow any exploration of the concepts of time and the future. A developing awareness of these issues remains crucial to young children, even when they are undertaking activities which do not appear on the surface to have any immediate bearing on the concepts as we understand them. By physically manipulating clay, for example, the child engages with the principles of desire, success, failure, expectation, effort and satisfaction, all of which have been identified as fundamental bases for an understanding of the future (Piaget 1955: 321, 347).

This tangibly direct means of engaging with concepts accords, in turn, with the close correlation in younger children between a developing sense of time and physical development. Wallis, for example, has noted that the time spent by babies crawling across distances in order to reach a desired object helps give rise to their internal sense of time (R. Wallis 'Le Temps, quatrième dimension de l'esprit', 1966, cited in Whitrow 1980: 68). The act of crawling helps babies to begin to understand the relationship between distance, antic- ipated time and satisfaction. The interrelations between motion and desire and a growing understanding of external temporal sequences will continue to develop in line with children's ongoing developmental experiences. They are still present in the four- and five-year-olds' emphasis on physically manipulating objects in order to gain control over the environment.

As children engage actively with the environment, they store, retrieve and combine fragments of information which subsequently form the basis of their developing concepts (Green 1975: 1). As Toffler has emphasised, active learning enables children to feel connected to the environment by allowing them to feel that they have gained some sense of control over the outside world (Toffler 1974: 16–18). This method of processing time should not be undervalued because it does not conform to an adult understanding. The principle of active learning demonstrates the extent to which young children strive constantly to make sense of their place in the world by reframing concepts in terms of their connectedness with them. The early childhood professional should take children's conceptual frameworks seriously and attempt to devise curricula which support and extend the futures-oriented aspects of their thinking.

Aims and methods of research

Having established the fundamental appropriateness of exploring the issue of time with young children, it is nonetheless clear that four- and five-year- olds' understandings of the future require further clarification. Are young children alienated from the future to the same degree as older students? To what extent are the developmental characteristics outlined above influenced by external and social factors? What is the role of fantasy and role playing? How, if at all, does convention impinge on imagination?

To begin to answer these questions, it is necessary to listen to the testi- monies of young children as a means of counter-balancing the previous adult-centred theoretical account of child development and the notion of time. By allowing the children to speak for themselves, we might gain a better understanding of some of the ways in which they make sense of the concept of the future and their place in it. The following research draws on 40 interviews with four- and five-year-old children attending two centres, one sessional and one extended hours, the first situated at a university but funded as a local community kindergarten and the other attached to a university department, but situated off-campus and accessed equally by the local community. The children's ages ranged from four years and five months to five years and ten months. The research focus was qualitative in nature and involved asking individual children at the outset of the interview what the future meant to them. The children were then asked to draw a picture of themselves as adults and another picture of what the world would be like when they are adults. No visual stimulus was provided during the interviews to guide or direct discussions or drawings.

Allowing children to speak for themselves enables us to begin to understand something of the extraordinary vitality and diversity which is so characteristic of their understandings of the concept of the future and their place within it. Their comments along these lines will also contrast strikingly with the negativity encountered in the older children's attitudes to the future just as they will establish clearly the relevance and need for a consideration of the future in any forward thinking educational curriculum.

Research findings

The previous discussion has highlighted in general terms a divergence between pre-school children's understandings of time and those of adults. This holds true equally for a group of pre-school children interviewed for this study on the topic of the future. Over half were unable to offer a definition of the future (although they were able to explore the concept, as shall presently be discussed). Those who did varied greatly in their understandings of what it constituted. Only a very few were able to define the future according to an adult's conventional framework. One child, for example defined the future as 'Something that will help, that's going to happen to you a bit later in life' (female, five years and ten months). This child also associated age with difference. Things around her in the world in the future will be different because 'They'll be a bit old.' Another child referred to the future as 'some time forward' (male, four years and ten months). For him the future was a place in which new ideas could be put into action: 'Better ideas might make fire-engines better.' Another child equated the future with the concept of growth: 'The future means that it's something not in our life, when another life, when your kids grow up. Then starts a new future' (male, five years and six months). The child's subsequent discussion revealed the future as a time in which he could enjoy many inventions 'the future is [a] thing not like nowadays like a car could turn and fly and stuff like that' (Figure 1).

The pre-school children interviewed commonly connected the concept of the future with the concept of growth. Their understanding of what this future growth entailed nonetheless varied greatly, as did their understanding of how the future might relate to other concepts of growth and development. Some children understood that the future was located within the time scale, but they framed it in terms of the past: 'It means it has gone. Because

Figure I   'The future is [a] thing not like nowadays like a car could turn and fly and stuff like that' (male, five years and six months)

that day has gone' (female, five years and four months). Another child inter-wove his discussion of the future freely between the past and the future: 'It means the day is past. In the future the video of the future ... they will fly motorbikes' (male, five years). Another child described the future as: 'It's what happened with your life' (female, four years and ten months). This child was, at the same time, able to move into the future tense when answering the question of what she would do when she grew up. Yet she again reverted to the past tense when discussing what the world would be like in the future. Her subsequent discussion interwove the past with the present and the future into a discussion of the global future which constantly drew upon her own knowledge and personal interests to build upon a developing understanding of the concept:

They had different coloured flowers and leaves and twisters like Dorothy [in *The Wizard of Oz*]. And did you know in the olden days they had a twist a twister? It could even blow the sun away. You saw the blue air. It was very lovely in the olden days. But when it got so old and the builders came around and God made the trees and things and then we had the country and the city. And instead of the olden days they had this lovely [pause]. And then all the other worlds were poor and some were not. That's what it looks like in the olden days. When it got very old they didn't have this colourful world. They just had all different yucky things like they had gun shooting, like this. They had. And they were fighting each other and then everybody is killed and [pause]. Well this is another world like here. Some builders heard it someone told them that we should make another world, so they did, and had it like this. There was cities and all sorts of things … You know this whole life up in the sky there is all different and the news follows what little things that they can find out what's happening tomorrow afternoon or what little things.

(female, four years and ten months, see Figure 2)

This child's understanding of the future is clearly under-developed from an adult perspective. Yet her comments underline that she has, nonetheless, been engaging keenly with the concept from within her own fluid and constantly evolving point of view. Her understanding of the future results from an ability to combine, in a highly creative and synthetic manner, a complete world of her own from a diverse variety of sources, ranging from *The Wizard of Oz* to the Bible and news reportage. She was able to connect the global emphasis of television news with its futures-perspective ('the news follows what little things that they can find out what's happening tomorrow') and to make the link between this understanding and the universal, cosmic perspective of Old Testament narrative ('God's building in the olden days'). She was even able to add to this a nascent understanding of social justice issues ('all the other worlds were poor and some were not').

Figure 2   'Well this is another world like here. Some builders heard it someone told them that we should make another world, so they did' (female, four years and ten months)

Unifying these diverse and disparate sources of interest was the sheer conviction of this child's imaginative fantasy. Fantasy gave her the agency to maintain complete creative control during all stages of the interview. At one point, for example, she conjured up a vision of guns and humans 'fighting each other and then everybody is killed'. Before this was allowed to develop into a threateningly negative theme in the narrative, however, she effortlessly and decisively switched her attention to the creation of a new world ('Well this is another world like here. Some builders heard it someone told them that we should make another world, so they did'). The sense of control and imaginative freedom manifested in these comments stands in stark contrast to the conventionalised, negative expressions of the future outlined by the older children.

Personally relevant global futures

When asked to describe what the world would be like in the future, the children were consistent in their desire to render the global perspective of the future meaningful to their own experiences and outlooks. For three children, this meant drawing Australia, with two also drawing their home town of Melbourne (female, five years and four months; male, five years and six months; male, five years and two months). For others, it meant defining the future as a place where they would enjoy their favourite activities such as fishing, roller-blading and going to gymbaroo, riding bikes, watching favourite television programmes (Figure 3).

More complex elaborations on personally relevant perspectives of the world were also possible. One child drew Kangaroo Island alongside Australia and Melbourne. This had a personal relevance since he had recently gone to Kangaroo Island on vacation (male, five years and two months). Another child redefined the concept of the world, noting that 'There's one big world. There's lots of little planets on it' (male, five years and six months). The child did not wish to explore the broader implications of this concept of planets within planets, presumably because it offered little scope for personal identification. The concept was visualised, instead, in directly immediate terms. His home town of Melbourne became the biggest planet before the concept moved to a more personally interesting image of tropical islands with palm trees, ships, water and sharks. At this point, the child's interest in the exploration of the fantasy at hand took over and the global vision of the future was momentarily eclipsed by an elaboration on the theme of ships and sharks.

All the children exercised a comparable freedom and flexibility over their often protean visions of the future. This flexibility extended to their ideas of what they might do in the future. One child, for example, progressed in his discussion of his future life from being a soldier, to an ambulance driver and then to a racing car driver (male, five years and six months). The progression

Figure 3 'In the future I am going to ride a bike' (female, five years and two months)

of ideas was dictated as much by visual concerns as it was guided logically and conceptually since, by discussing the details in his drawings, he triggered his memory and refined his understandings so that they could incorporate new ideas.

Many of the interviews demonstrated a strong awareness of the global aspect of the future. This was evident, for example, in the statements of a child who was not able to define the future, but was, nonetheless, able to describe the term as meaning 'To keep the world umm, to keep the world, umm, umm, umm' (female, four years and eleven months). Other children used a global analogy to define the future as 'the world, like nature, or cities' (male, five years and six months, see Figure 4) and 'The future could save the world maybe' (male, four years and eleven months). For a number of those interviewed this global perspective lent itself to an awareness of ecological issues. One child, for example, commented that there will be no trees in the future because 'they use them all for work' (female, five years and eight months). Another child, who was initially unable to define the future, used environmental issues to trigger an exploration of the global orientation of the future. When asked what he wanted to be when he grew up, he replied that he would like to:

Make something, make something, something turn on the dark pollution in the sea in to more of the same thing, to more food, and then you won't have all the pollution in the sea. Then I would make an underground tunnel for it to go through and then I think the trucks.

(male, four years and eleven months)

This child's engagement with the problem of environmental destruction differs markedly from the older children's commentaries on environmental concerns. In contrast to the disempowering feelings experienced by the older children, this child perceives the problem of pollution in the context of its solution as a result of the force and ingenuity of his futures-oriented creativity. As a further demonstration of this, he extended the vision, in the next breath, so that it could incorporate additional feats of engineering. These future inventions, moreover, held a personal relevance to the child since they reflected his recent visit to England, with its recently opened Channel tunnel. Everything in the future is possible for this child since the future will provide him full scope for his incipient powers of creativity and problem-solving.

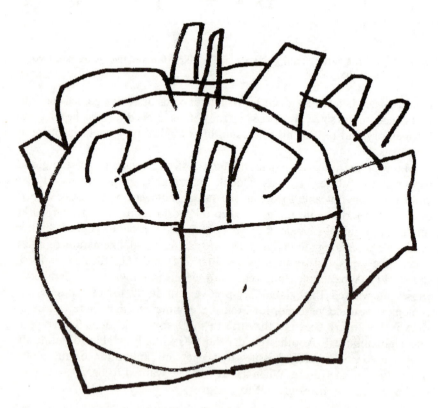

Figure 4   'The world, like nature, or cities' (male, five years and six months)

A number of the children utilised a comparable emphasis on exploring ecological and health issues via the medium of creative inventions for solving problems. One child, for example, was interested in making a machine that could 'shrink things [like] ... rubbish' so that there would be less rubbish in the world: 'First we would see what would be good to recycle and what wouldn't like glass bottles they might break, tin cans they're ok ... shrink all the other things' (male, five years and six months, see Figure 5). This child's environmental understanding was evident throughout his interview: 'If you chopped all of them down you wouldn't be able to breathe would we?'

One of the most striking features of the interviews was the manner in which the children were able to draw freely on the global dimension of the future as a means of encompassing disparate and occasionally negative images of the future within a positive and personally meaningful framework. The global was made relevant, for these children, by being interconnected with the personal, and the negative, or the unsettling, was overturned by its being interconnected with the positive. Two children, for

Figure 5   'First we would see what would be good to recycle and what wouldn't' (male, five years and six months)

example, mentioned Bosnia. This must have entered their consciousness through news items on the traumas of the then-recent Serbo-Croatian war. But the negative and incomprehensibly complex 'global' associations of this imagery were neutralised by its being grouped with positive and personally relevant images. The previously discussed child, for example, drew Bosnia alongside Australia, Melbourne and Kangaroo Island (male, five years and three months). He demonstrated a similar control over his creation as the child who overcame the potentially unsettling elements of her negative fantasy by replacing them with a new and positive creation.

In this and other examples the children's images of the future can be seen to have been frequently influenced by the mass media. One child, for example, wanted to be 'a rock star like Michael Jackson' when he grew up (male, four years and eleven months), while others identified other role models such as Luke Skywalker (male, five years and six months). Another framed her understanding of the future more fundamentally within the terms of reference set up by the futuristic television series *Dr Who*: 'When Doctor Who was alive ... we will be alive in the future' (female, five years). We have also noted the number of children who commented on environmental issues attached to the future.

There is a striking contrast to be noted here between these mass media influences and the discussions of the future by the older children. In the pre-school children's comments, the conventional imagery of the mass media remains wholly subordinate to the children's own perspectives. It forms one element in a rich array of source materials which are to be transformed into a new synthesis by the force of the children's flexibility and creativity. Thus the 'island' of Bosnia, drawn by one child alongside Melbourne, Australia and Kangaroo Island, was placed beneath a freely associative fantasy of stairs leading from the world into a vision of a space inhabited by monkeys and aliens (male, five years and three months, see Figure 6). The conventional and the negative are here cancelled out by their being almost literally overwhelmed by the energy and positivity of the child's fantasy. Another child's discussion of what he would do in the future involved Saddam Hussein and the Gulf War: 'I told my mum I want to grow up and save the world and fight the Arabian Knights, Saddam Hussein, his army and the pirates' (male, five years and three months, see Figure 7). Yet this child was able to combine a source of media inspiration with personal play experiences and related associations set up by other personal and idiosyncratic 'Arabian' points of reference. At one stage he referred to his mother buying him a rope to play games which related back, in turn, to his reading of Aladdin and the Arabian Knights: 'I just tell my friends to go in the back way with the man and go up the very top of the Arabian Knight castle and to be holding the rope and then throw it down to me and I'll climb up it.' The descriptions of the future by older children, by contrast, remained frequently locked within a received framework of conventional, dystopian science fiction imagery, as we have seen. The difference in the level of creative freedom and control is acute. The task of the early childhood professional should be to keep the empowering focus of this perspective open, as much as possible, by extending and framing it within the curriculum.

The concepts of growth and change and continuity

The children consistently addressed the future through the framework of growth: 'and the children grow up' (male, four years and eleven months) and 'Well, I'm going to be older' (male, five years) and 'I'll be a bit bigger than normal' (male, four years and ten months) and ' My feet will be bigger' (female, five years and two months) and 'My clothes are going to be bigger' (female, four years and seven months). As was previously discussed, most of them equated the future with being older, although the diversity of the ages identified as being old provides a further indication of their loosely defined understandings of the 'adult' measurement of time. For one child, attending school meant being an adult (female, four years and eleven months). For others, the ages identified as being grown up ranged from six, to seventeen,

Figure 6   'Kangaroo Island, Bosnia and monkeys in space' (male, five years and three months)

Figure 7   'I want to grow up and save the world' (male, five years and three
           months)

to twenty-two, to sixty (male, five years and two months; female, five years
and four months; male, four years and eleven months; male, four years and
five months). This fluidity of understanding of age correlates with other
recent studies of children's understanding of time (Scott 1998: 9).

   One of the attractions of growing older for these children was that it
would enable them to exercise an increased level of understanding and
control over the world. For one child being older meant he would be able to
kill a monster 'because I'm sixty-one ... I'll be able to kill him. I'm more
than him, I'll be sixty-two' (male, four years and five months). Another
child's understanding of the future involved a recognition of the limitations
inherent in her level of understanding in the present. For her, the future
would be when she went to school and learned 'lots of things that you can't
understand when you're a little kid' (female, five years and six months). This
child was able to stand back from her own development and express a belief
in the principle that being grown up means 'you sort of get more truthful
and things'. Her sense of the difficult, abstract nature of the process of

getting 'more truthful and things' was, nonetheless made more personally understandable and attainable by the fact that it was going to occur when she attended school and also by the fact that her framing of the concept was influenced by her recent identification with the fictional character of Pippy Longstocking. The process of combining the global with the personal and the fantastic with the real enabled the children to gain a sense of direct access to the global aspects of future time. Another child linked a comparable understanding of the future through the concept of growth: 'there might be more fish, because the grown up fish might have, their eggs might have hatched more' (male, five years and six months). Another child saw the concept of growth in purely physical terms when he stated that the Westgate bridge, which his parents frequently travelled over, would be smaller because he would be bigger (male, five years).

Change and continuity constituted another key framework through which many of the children explored the concept of the future. This progressed from a recognition of difference in age to an understanding of the way in which the world would change in the future. One child, for example, believed the world of the future would be different because the bark on trees would change with age and 'the new trees would grow' (female, five years). A similar metaphor was adopted by another child, who noted that the trees in the future will look older because they will have 'scratches' on them. They will also lose their leaves and grow tall (female, five years and ten months, see Figure 8). These children were able to negotiate the abstract nature of future change, once again, by expressing it in terms that were tangible and that had direct applications to their everyday experiences. A similar understanding was contained in another child's comment that the world was going to be different in the future because 'houses will be changed. Because I saw people making them and making some houses up near [his sibling's] school and they got different and different and different' (male, four years and eleven months).

Unlike their older counterparts, the younger children interviewed understood that the future held a number of possibilities for personal choice. One child noted, for example, that he 'might have kids. Or I might not have them. I might find a job, but I don't know what I am going to be yet. I'm going to wait until I'm grown up' (male, five years and six months). Another child saw the future as a series of career choices which also allowed for complex understandings of differences of perception about the future in the past: 'First I wanted to be a ranger, then I wanted to be an acrobat and now I want to be. Well I want to be a person which looks after the horses and gives people rides on them' (female, five years). A sense of choice was particularly striking in one child's recognition that she still has plenty of time to change her mind in the future: 'I'm going swimming in October first. Then I'm going to France. After that we haven't made up our minds' (female, five years). This child understood the future to be something that she and her mother would construct at their own leisure, some time after swimming lessons and their impending overseas trip.

Research conclusions

These interviews highlight the difficulty experienced by most four- and five-year-old children when called upon to define the future from an adult perspective. Only a small proportion of the children were able to demonstrate a clear understanding of the future as a temporal location or space, with some children viewing it in terms of the past. Even so, all the children interviewed were nonetheless able to project themselves into a vision of what they would be like when they grew up. Their world of the future offered them the possibility to explore different scenarios, some fantastic, some imaginative, some based on their understanding of adults' lives and some based on storybook and movie role-models.

Most of the children acknowledged that 'grown up' involved a time where things change or are different because of the passing of time and their own

Figure 8   'The trees in the future will look older' (female, five years and ten months)

active engagement within this period of change. Thus one child discussed the future within the framework of a historical progression of time: 'Like first it would be like it was dinosaurs but then like this' (female, five years and six months). For other children this progression of time would be more immediate to life experiences: 'Something else happens ... like when I go to school. That's the future' (male, five years and one month). One child equated the progression of time to a journey: 'Somewhere where you go' (male, five years and seven months) and then later in the discussion: 'because it's a long time 'til I'm an adult'. Another child stated that in the future her mother would be a grandmother because she would be a mother (female, five years and three months). Along similar lines, one child noted that in the future he 'won't be at kinder but Adam will, he's my little brother' (male five years). Another child conceived the future as a series of contiguous events: 'First I'm going to be a sister. Then I'll be an adult and go to work. I think I might get married. I will go overseas and see lots of new places' (female, five years). This child was clearly aware that each level of her personal development fed into the other and played a causative role on her progression towards the next stage.

For all the children it was a time in which they would be able to exert control over whatever scenario came to hand. Whether it was mooring a boat, driving parents in a car, understanding concepts at school that are too difficult to understand now, or looking after people and inventing new medical devices, the future was consistently interpreted in positive terms by the children as a time in which ideas will be put into action. It was obvious from what they expressed that the children felt positively connected to the world outside since it could still be, in some way, their world. The boundaries of what is immediate and personally relevant and what is remote and abstract have not yet been drawn for these children.

A familiarity with wider social concerns was also strikingly evident throughout the children's comments. The children were clearly engaged by current issues of pollution, the environment, contemporary music and warfare and they used their knowledge of these and other issues in new contexts in order to understand them more fully and recast them in a manner which was more meaningful to them. The interviews provided the children with another means of testing their knowledge and understandings. They indicate the need for early childhood professionals to develop strategies to encourage and sustain the children's examination of such concepts throughout the year. They also indicate the need for an educational and philosophical framework to give additional shape and developmental reference to these dynamic and protean understandings. It is worth while, therefore, exploring an appropriate methodology for making sense of time and the future before directing our attention to more detailed curricula applications.

Chapter 3

Futures studies

A catalyst for social and educational change

> We are no longer dealing with isolated sequences of events, separable in time ... There is a vastly greater simultaneity of occurrence, swifter interpenetration, and increased feedback of one set of changes upon another ... In effect, the scale of these changes has already altered many of the ground rules which have hitherto governed and defined the human condition.
>
> (MacHale 1973: 13)

From the earliest stage of development we expend much of our energies learning to adapt to change and cope with its many different contexts. Our quality of life is often directly contingent on the extent to which we succeed in accomplishing this often challenging task. Much of the anxiety registered in the discussion of young people's attitudes stems from an anxiety towards change now and in the future and its attendant uncertainty. What will we be doing in ten years time? How will we fit into society? What skills will we need to function successfully in the world of the future? The future is a volatile factor in our lives because it represents the unknown. We cannot be certain what it will hold for us.

The prospect of change into the future can appear particularly unsettling given our current position in history. The speed and rapidity of change which so characterised the technological and conceptual developments of the twentieth century has necessitated a radical redefinition of the scope and nature of social and cultural change. The contrast between the rate of pre- and post-twentieth-century change has been variously characterised by the equation 'that the next three decades will bring at least two centuries' worth of change, as measured in historical terms' and by the projection that 'the next hundred years is likely to exceed the previous thousand years in the impact, speed, scope and importance of its changes' (L. Brown, 'Futuristics and Education: An ASCD Task Force Report', 1979, cited in Benjamin 1989: 8; Beare and Slaughter 1993: 5).

This framework of dynamic and increasing change radically alters the conventionally fixed perspective of the horizon of the future from its viewing point in the present. The perspective of time no longer presents any fixed points of reference. Both the horizon and the viewpoint are constantly shifting as one set of circumstances rapidly gives way to a new and unexpected set of conditions, as, for example, when a new form of technology renders previous technology obsolete within a short period of time. As we saw in the young people's commentaries, the increasing rapidity of change constitutes a major source of anxiety for the future.

The discipline of futures studies seeks to formulate frameworks for discussion of futures-related issues which are responsive to this dynamic and complex reality. Futures studies emerged after the Second World War as a movement uniting the interests of a diverse range of philosophical and educational researchers. It developed initially out of a concern for the devastating impact of the war and sought to help avert the possibility of another global tragedy by developing a more forward-looking agenda. Since then it has grown increasingly to incorporate secondary and tertiary educational studies.

Futures studies recognises that the speed and rapidity of modern change contributes towards a common sense of alienation and is concerned with the need to develop in individuals an understanding of the complex processes of change and the ability to think in a dynamic and flexible way about the future. The fundamental objective of futures studies is to develop the ability within individuals to control and direct their own futures. Futures studies aims to encourage individuals not to fear change, but rather to feel that they can manipulate and influence events directly and that, through this, they can create change rather than suffer it.

The limitations of forecasting

This undertaking involves futures studies researchers in a critique of the limitations inherent within many of the conventional frameworks used for understanding concepts of time. One such framework is the practice of forecasting. It is a natural urge of humanity to anticipate the future, to project ourselves into the future and to plan our present accordingly. This is commonly done by attempting to construct forecasts of what the future will be like. The usefulness of this method is severely limited by the fact that we can never be certain what the future will hold and so forecasting can never be more than speculation or educated guesswork (Slaughter 1986: 17). It is for this reason that forecasts of the future are so often incorrect.

A good illustration of this comes in an article published in a war-time popular science magazine. In 1940, the readers of *Modern World* were informed of the possibility that one day rockets could fly to the moon. The scientist, Dr Lombard, stressed that this would not happen until some time in the future, only after rockets had been invented which could fly through the stratosphere 'taking passengers around the world at speeds exceeding 1,000 miles per hour'. 'Success is not just around the corner in these

researches', Dr Lombard stated, 'but we know we are on a track that is
leading somewhere. Time will tell how successful we have been. Meanwhile,
we dare to dream anyway.' Dr Lombard could not conceive of putting a date
on the time at which his dream would become a reality. He had no way of
knowing, of course, that rockets would be sent into space a mere decade
after his words and that men would land on the moon less than two decades
later, all well before the invention of passenger rockets.

This example underscores the unknowable aspect of the future and the
difficulties experienced by individuals when they attempt to predict what the
future will hold. There are many memorable examples of the limitations
involved in the forecasting approach to the future. The gleaming city of
Metropolis in the Fritz Lang movie of the same name, for example, contains
an incongruous mixture of futuristic images of suspended walkways and
antiquated biplanes. Such images tend to date quickly. Fritz Lang's
Metropolis can now be classified without difficulty as a product of the
1920s. It holds considerable power as an expressionist and art-deco fantasy,
but very little credibility as a realistic forecast of the future. The forecasting
approach to the future thus fails because it attempts to impose a singular
version of events onto the future. Such an approach can never be true to
reality since it does not allow for the many possible outcomes in the future
as well as for the diversity of opinions and situations existing within any
period.

Skills for the future: foresight and critical thinking

As an alternative to the forecasting approach to the future, futures studies
seeks to develop ways of thinking that will equip individuals for the future.
The skills identified as important in this regard include imagination and
creativity, inventiveness, independent critical thinking, foresight and projection, decision-making, the ability to grasp connections between seemingly
disparate phenomena and the ability to deal with surprise, conflict and irres-
olution (Goodlad 1973: 220; Tinkler 1987: 4; Beare and Slaughter 1993:
114–15).

Foresight has been particularly stressed by commentators. Richard
Slaughter defines foresight as 'a conscious effort to expand awareness and to
clarify the dynamics of emerging situations' (Slaughter 1990b:1). Foresight
is distinguished from forecasting by its emphasis on the contemplation of a
range of options for the future rather than a fixed, singular ideal. It assists
individuals to extend their thinking beyond the present and to assess
possible consequences, to anticipate problems and to think through implications of future-related events. These thought processes create what Slaughter
terms a 'decision context' in which the individual can act upon future-
related issues with a flexibility that will allow for adaptation to suit future
contingencies. One way of framing this process is to develop concepts of

probable, possible and preferable options for the future. The usefulness of a framework of this kind lies in the manner in which it encourages individuals to develop an awareness of how to act on issues (Gough 1989: 54). The term 'futures studies' recognises, in itself, the many options which are available for the future. It presents itself through its title as an alternative to the traditional belief that the complex possibilities for the future can or should be reduced to a single definable end goal or outcome.

The quality of critical thinking is closely related to foresight. This involves individuals in a process of critical engaging with the commonly taken-for-granted mores and conventions of society. Critical thinking enables individuals to see and to question the social frameworks which order and, at times, delimit the parameters of life. Once individuals have recognised the underlying structures influencing the construction of their lives, they can begin to devise means and methods of questioning them rather than taking them for granted as permanent and immovable fixtures of existence. The process of thinking these issues through will involve them in countering short-term solutions to problems with an understanding of their broader social significance (Slaughter 1991b: 29–34).

Adherents of futures studies stress the degree to which the development of these skills will assist individuals not only in the future, but also in the here and now of the present. They seek to provide a forum for individuals to affirm their connections with the outside world of culture, society and the environment (Gay 1981: 81). Once individuals acknowledge their common relation to the future they can begin to examine ways in which they are not isolated and passive recipients of change but, rather, are linked with others in the common project of becoming autonomous and active creators of the future. The development of skills of this kind is interpreted as being of potentially great benefit since they encourage a positive self-concept and a sense of connectedness with the outside world, qualities which are evidently missing from the previously discussed young people's comments on the future. An undertaking of this kind should, rather, encourage individuals:

> to develop a rich network of linkages between their own life-structures and the wider problems and dimensions of change which underlie and support (or threaten) them. To engage with wider processes makes it possible to retain greater control over one's life and even to exert a shaping influence within the wider context.
>
> (Slaughter 1985: 5)

The relationship between past, present and future

Futures studies researchers are also concerned to look beyond the limitations inherent within the conventional separation of time into past, present and future. This convention is useful in so far as it enables individuals to gain a

concrete perspective on the abstract nature of time by distinguishing themselves from what has come and what will be. But this understanding of time
is also limited by the fact that it presents a falsely schematic view of the
continuities inherent within the time-scale.

The process of isolating moments into different positions on the time-
scale encourages an understanding of time as a linear progression which
bears little relation to its fluidity and the dynamic nature of change
(Slaughter 1985: 54). Implicit within this concept of linear progression is an
ideal model which views the passage of time as a logical progression of
linked events towards a resolved conclusion. This artificial and unrealistic
imposition of a framework of logic upon the randomness of time is often
informed by an essentially moralistic vision of historical development. This
perspective interprets history as being governed by the principle of progress,
according to which every event represents a step either forward or backward in a progress towards a definable ideal. A related venerable yet still
common way of framing this moralising approach is to adopt a biological
metaphor as a means of understanding historical development. A classic
example of this kind of approach is the interpretation of historical development in terms of the metaphor of growth from unsophisticated origins to
brilliant and fully resolved maturity and thence to decadent and enfeebled
old age.

A further limitation of the division of time into past, present and future
is that it encourages a perception of the present as somehow separate from
the past and from the future. This 'temporal chauvinism', as one writer has
described it, fails to recognise the way in which past, present and future are
linked within a continuum (Gough 1987b: 3). It can result in a lack of an
awareness of the relevance of the future to the present so that the future
comes to be perceived as a remote and alien zone, the effects of which have
been charted in the previously discussed attitudes of young people to the
future. The conventional, dystopian imagery drawn upon by many of these
young people indicates that they have become, in this respect at least, largely
passive receptors of a cultural viewpoint formulated by others rather than
creators of their own perceptions of the future. Adherents of futures studies
would endeavour to provide frameworks of understanding that might help
these individuals to appreciate their connection with the future and, thus,
the extent to which they are responsible for its creation.

Futures studies offers an alternative to these traditional interpretations of
time. It views past, present and future as inextricably linked together.
Slaughter illustrates this diagrammatically. Rather than viewing time periods
as distinct, he sees them as feeding into each other as part of a fluid
continuum. To view the relationship between past, present and future in this
manner is to begin to recognise the degree to which the present is directly
influenced by our understanding of the future. This approach to understanding time also recognises that our decisions are influenced by an

understanding of what we have experienced in the past. Futures studies accordingly helps individuals to understand the extent to which their decisions in the present will be shaped by their feelings, hopes, aspirations and fears towards the future (Gough 1990b: 300). The future, when viewed from this perspective, is no longer an abstract and remote zone with little direct bearing on individuals' lives. It becomes, rather, a force whose presence is felt every day influencing all our actions and decisions in a most direct and immediate way.

Elise Boulding conceives time in a manner which is commensurate with these objectives. She reorganises the present into a time frame of 200 years in recognition of the importance of reflecting on the past and the future while considering our actions in the present (Boulding 1989: 28–9). Slaughter has represented this idea of a 200-year present as a diagrammatic family chain. Placing people at the forefront of the time frame highlights the fluidity of time through generations and the extent to which individuals are bound together through time by cultural processes such as belief systems, mores, traditions, institutions, customs and values. The diagram helps the individuals to reflect upon their personal experiences and to visualise the parameters of short- and long-term thinking. The family framework emphasises the relative impact of each individual in human terms. It also illustrates how meanings attached to specific time-frames can influence our perceptions of past, present and future. Boulding has created a framework which illustrates how the measurement of time is not restricted by physical terms. It can encompass and sustain time and space as far as the mind can conceive, thus drawing out the abilities of creativity and imagination which are frequently emphasised by futures studies researchers.

Symbols

The discussion thus far has stressed in a general sense the importance of social and cultural analysis as a means of understanding some of the reasons for the ways in which individuals perceive time and as a means of providing them with a critical methodology to better understand and prepare for the future. Symbols provide a vitally important index of the aspirations of the cultures which generate them. They are both symptomatic of the attitudes towards the future outlined above as well as a potential source of renewal for reconceptualising and reframing issues relating to the future. Futures studies frequently stresses its potential to reorient our attitudes to the future (Polak 1961: passim; Boulding 1973: 76–101, 1989: 24–9; Slaughter 1991a: 499–515).

Symbols convey generalised meaning. A symbol communicates meaning beyond itself to signify broader, often abstract or philosophical, cultural principles and beliefs. They have served this function since earliest times. In the Neolithic period, for instance, sculpted fertility goddesses acted as good luck charms for the continuation of plentiful crops and harvests. The sculpted goddesses acted as reference points to the wider concerns, hopes and aspirations of the people using them by expressing confidence in the community and its ability to survive and prosper into the next season (Fingersten 1970: 129).

From the time of their earliest usage symbols have thus played an important role in the construction and reinforcement of belief systems. By understanding and identifying with a symbolic representation the individual shared in the construction of the belief system to which the symbol referred. The individual, in effect, committed him or herself to a belief in the wider ideology to which the symbol contributed. Symbols have thus played a significant role in bonding communities together through their belief systems and in galvanising them against opposing cultures and ideologies. A particularly clear example of this function of symbolism comes in the project of Counter-Reformation art. During this period, in Italy from the mid- to the late sixteenth century, an attempt was made to reform Roman Catholic art in order to reaffirm and strengthen Catholicism against the perceived heresy of northern European Protestantism (Blunt 1962: 103–36).

A fundamental role of symbolism, therefore, is to reinforce a consensus of belief and, in so doing, to bind cultures together through their ideologies. This function is particularly evident in western European art of the thirteenth to sixteenth centuries. During this period symbols were developed in order to explain and reinforce a unified religious belief system whose meanings were understood through long tradition. Coming at the end of that tradition, the Renaissance mind instantly identified with and understood that an image of a female figure standing on a dragon symbolised St Margaret of Antioch because it shared in the religious belief system and world-view to which her image belonged. It distinguished, moreover, between St Margaret of Antioch and St Martha one of whose attributes is also a dragon, because of their differing supplementary attributes. St Margaret of Antioch holds the martyr's palm and Cross while St Martha holds a vessel of holy water and an aspergillum (Hall 1974: 34, 198, 201).

This distinction underlines that the success of symbols is partly based upon the manner in which they give immediately relevant visual form to a wider framework of belief. St Margaret of Antioch's legend tells of her refusal to marry the prefect of Antioch because she wished to remain a Christian virgin. She was subsequently tortured, thrown into a dungeon and devoured by Satan in the form of a dragon. The Cross which she carried with her saved her from the dragon, causing the dragon to spew her forth unharmed. The symbols of the martyr's palm and the Cross thus serve both to highlight the significant narrative aspects of her story as well as to remain relevant within the wider framework of martyrdom and the strength of Christian faith which her story underlines.

St Margaret's significance in the wider belief system would always have been explained in accordance with the didactic function of medieval and Renaissance religious art. The lives of the saints throw light on the wider significance of Christian belief as they serve as an example to humanity and their exalted position enables them to act as intermediaries between man and God. The words 'Orate pro nobis' (pray for us) which are repeated by the faithful in the litany of the saints during the Catholic Mass underline this and this wider meaning would have instantly sprung to the mind of a Renaissance viewer contemplating an image of a saint.

Contemporary symbols, however, serve a number of fundamentally different functions. Renaissance symbols were used to explain and reinforce a unified religious belief system. The Renaissance mind would have instantly identified with and understood that an image of a female figure standing on a dragon symbolised St Margaret of Antioch because it shared in the world-view to which her image belonged. The contemporary viewer, on the other hand, would have difficulty appreciating the significance of this image for two reasons. First, we live in a vastly different world from that of 500 years ago when the symbols examined today by the discipline of iconography were the cultural norm. A unified Christian doctrine is no longer possible as the dominant world-view and it has been replaced by a number of alternative belief systems. The function and content of imagery and symbols have also changed over the past several hundred years.

There is not the same degree of consensus with regard to contemporary symbols as there was with regard to Renaissance symbols. Instead, they represent a number of only partially integrated concepts, such as wealth, taste, discrimination and power. There is a fundamental distinction between an image of St Margaret of Antioch and a contemporary symbol, such as the previously discussed advertisement of the sleek red sports car. The image of St Margaret refers to a network of symbolic images each of which contributes towards explaining a cohesive, consensus-based moral belief system. The car also refers to a belief system. It relates to the culture of late twentieth-century capitalism. But the distinction here is that there is not the same degree of consensus about that belief system and how it is to be symbolised. There is no single authorised text or gospel of late twentieth-century capitalism, and it is not the dominant orthodoxy of modern-day belief.

A lack of cohesion in contemporary symbolism is thus symptomatic of an uncohesive world-view. It is for this reason that futures studies frequently stresses the need for individuals to rediscover the power of symbols. The complexity and diversity of contemporary life may militate against our acceptance of the reductive aspects of a universal belief system like medieval Christianity. Nevertheless, individuals still have much to learn from the efficacy of the symbolic structures evolved by such belief systems.

Symbols can give vividly memorable form to complex concepts such as the future, and can assist individuals to recognise the links between the seemingly unrelated factors feeding into such concepts. Through the use of symbols, individuals can develop a series of scenarios with which to engage and explore possible options for their future lives (Slaughter 1991a: 499–500). Symbols can, in this respect, facilitate a sense of connection with the world. Individuals can manipulate images and concepts of future life as a means towards defining and identifying their roles in the future. This process can encourage them to regain some sense of active control over the future, a concept which is so frequently stressed as one of the fundamental objectives of futures studies. A critical usage of symbols could also have assisted the previously discussed young people to move beyond the alien and stereotypical frameworks encountered in their discussions of the global future. Symbols, in short, constitute an important forum in which differing outlooks on the future can be extended and where new or modified outlooks can be forged. They offer a starting point for an exploration of the means out of the intellectual and emotional quandary outlined in the young people's expressions about the future.

Conclusion: futures studies' relevance to early childhood education

The seemingly abstract nature of time constitutes one of the most challenging aspects involved in any attempt to understand the future. Futures studies offers frameworks to help individuals to engage actively and positively with time and its closely attendant corollaries of diversity and change. In the process, it encourages individuals to feel connected with the outside world of culture and society. The previously discussed research suggests that a split takes place between the pre- and early school years. At this moment children manifest many of the uncertainties towards the future highlighted in the research into young people's attitudes to the future. Early childhood educators, on the other hand, start with a pronounced advantage on these matters since pre-school children already possess many of the very attitudes which futures studies seeks to re-establish in older individuals. This was strongly evident in the interviews with pre-school children on their understandings of time and the future. As we saw, the responses confirmed that the future cannot be explored with pre-school children in the same manner in which it is discussed with older children and adults. Four- to five-year-old children have a fundamentally different attitude towards the future and attendant notions of time and change which should always be recognised in the curriculum.

Pre-school children of these interviews, nonetheless, have much to teach us, as those qualities which futures studies stresses as necessary for a positive understanding of the future are inherent in their make-up. Their flexibility of thought, their positive and constructive outlook on life, their sense of the continuity of time, their creativity and imagination and their sense of personal connection with the world are all qualities which futures studies seeks to instil in individuals. Most important is that they feel personally connected to the future to an extent that young adults are generally unable to achieve. Young children do not have to work, as adults do, to re-establish a meaningful connection between the seemingly abstract dimension of the future and their own concerns as individuals. They do not experience this problem since they do not perceive time in our terms. Their ego-centrism and emphasis on active learning should thus be viewed as positive factors. Young children's sense of personal connection with time enables them to exert a correspondingly greater sense of control over it than most adults. Since they regard time as 'belonging' to them, in the sense that it is in some way oriented towards their needs and desires, young children are better able to extend and manipulate time. They are freer to develop a more flexible understanding of time than adults, with a correspondingly greater emphasis on imaginative fantasies about the past and the future and a less rigid adherence to external time (Green 1975: 6).

> I suspect that the boundaries which we read upon time, which are constructs anyway, are not very real to young children. Yesterday, today and tomorrow just flow seamlessly into one another. They represent one expression of a view of time which sees time as boundless. There is a sense of flowing intuitively with time ... once it has gone it is very hard to re-establish that same sense of immersion in a flow.
>
> (Slaughter, interview with the author, 1989)

The challenge for early childhood educators is thus to bring out and place value on the natural qualities of children. The application of futures studies in the early childhood curriculum does not involve making pronouncements on life in the twenty-first century. It is, rather, about extending and encouraging the potential for growth and development which is indicated in the children's own words. In order for this to be achieved it will nonetheless be necessary first to consider the principles and application of futures studies in educational settings. An overview of futures education would have the additional benefit of bringing together the common points of reference shared across the educational spectrum which can then serve as a useful basis upon which to build an analysis of futures concerns in early childhood education.

Chapter 4

Futures studies and education

The education system has not, to date, responded well to the challenge of applying futures issues in pre-school to secondary educational curricula. This is partly attributable to the lack of an awareness on the part of most educators of the methodologies and philosophical orientations of futures studies. This gap in the educational knowledge base means that most educators do not possess the critical frameworks necessary to analyse perceptions of the future and to convert these concerns into practical learning experiences. In order to remedy this situation, futures researchers will need to continue the long-term objective of disseminating information about the discipline of futures studies across educational settings.

But while allowing for this lack of knowledge, the criticism can still justly be levelled that the education system has not adequately addressed its mission to provide children with the knowledge and skills to participate effectively in society now and in the future. Noel Gough has recently criticised the Australian education system for its lack of an adequate commitment to its future component. Gough has drawn attention to the manner in which educational researchers and policy-makers pay frequent lip service to the importance of preparing students for the future without, however, seriously addressing this as an objective in their curricula and in their methodologies (Gough 1990b: 299). According to Gough, the education system is characterised by a largely superficial understanding of futures issues. When addressed, the future is generally considered according to three sets of assumptions: the first, where futures are addressed tacitly in educational statements but not discussed in direct terms; the second, where a token reference to futures issues is used solely for rhetorical purposes; and the third, where taken-for-granted futures which utilise a predetermined version of the future as the basis for decision-making (Gough 1990b: 301–7, 1994: 11). Gough's conclusion that educational discourse relies too heavily on past and present analysis of issues has been echoed by Richard Slaughter and Headley Beare, who have warned of the consequences of an education system which replicates educative frameworks that are rooted in a sense of the past (Beare and Slaughter 1993: 102). Slaughter has gone so far as to caution that 'If education stays stubbornly locked into outdated paradigms and past perceptions of problems it becomes a source of social rigidity, not a remedy for it' (Slaughter 1986: 18).

Critical theorists stress the importance of educational institutions as transmitters of the dominant culture of society (Germov 1994: 2). The educational curriculum thus has the potential to play a major role in the development of young people's attitudes towards the future. Any deficiencies in its approach to the future will, accordingly, have a potentially significant, negative impact on young people's perceptions of the future. This was raised as a concern by the authors of the Social Education Survey, who examined the presentation of the future in Australian year ten secondary school texts. In these texts, the future was found to have been addressed according to a consistently negative framework which stressed social, economic and environmental problems without making due allowance for the potential of future generations to contribute energetically and creatively to solving problems (MacGregor 1989: 31–2). By reinforcing negative understandings of the future, these texts are thus perpetuating the previously articulated problem of young people's attitudes to the future, rather than helping to solve it.

The failings of this approach to education are rendered more apparent by the research undertaken in the 1970s which highlights the importance of students developing a positive and active approach to the future. An American study of 1977, for example, posits a correlation between an active orientation towards the future and higher levels of self-esteem and social responsibility (Allen and Plante 1980: 13). This research follows studies undertaken in the 1940s, 1950s and early 1960s in which a correlation was found to exist between high academic achievers, optimistic attitudes and a greater concern for future goals or a future time perspective (Teahan 1958: 379–80).

Some of these studies place special emphasis on the importance of an understanding of the future for an individual's development. Stinchcombe, for example, identifies an awareness of the future as the major factor distinguishing high school achievers from under-achievers (Stinchcombe, cited in Bell and Mau 1971: 33). Singer similarly stresses the significance of a future role image on children's social and educational development (Singer 1974: 19–32). Bell and Mau believe that a futures-focused image is the basis upon which to achieve social change (Bell and Mau 1971: 33). While these latter studies may run the risk of underestimating the formative influence of social and economic factors, there can be no doubting their conclusion that students who do not believe that the future will bring them anything will inevitably regard education as boring and irrelevant (Kauffman 1980: 74).

That students might themselves wish for a fuller exploration of futures issues in their curricula has been highlighted in a study undertaken in New Jersey in 1978 (Allen and Plante 1980: 111–12). Over 75 per cent of the 2,400 students interviewed identified the future as one of the main subjects requiring their study (1980: 111). The students' desire for a new curriculum perspective may, in part, be attributable to their dissatisfaction with the concerns of the traditional educational curriculum (Wilson 1989: 39). In this context, Allen and Plante, and Hutchinson, have all underlined the extent to which secondary school students frequently find the curriculum restrictive and irrelevant to their concerns (Allen and Plante 1980: 111–12; Hutchinson 1996: 80–1). The exploration of futures issues can thus offer students an avenue for exploring their hopes and fears in a more flexible and personally relevant manner than many of the traditional subjects that make up educational curricula.

There can thus be no doubting the real need which exists for the incorporation of futures-based components in educational curricula. The studies of young people's attitudes towards the future, of the importance of a positive sense of the future and of the failings of the education system to address these issues render this conclusion clear. But how are these issues to be addressed? What should the objectives of such a curriculum be and how should they be framed? To answer these questions we need to examine more closely the principles of futures studies as they are applied in educational contexts.

This task is rendered difficult by the fact that the study of futures in education remains a developing and relatively under-researched area. As Slaughter has underlined, little synthesis and comparative evaluation of futures in education has taken place (Slaughter 1989c: 16–17, 1991c: 14–15). The following discussion will thus build upon the growing body of research and literature which seeks to draw together, from a disparate range of sources and initiatives, the underlying tenets of futures studies as they are applied in education. These tenets can then act as a basis from which to address specific educational initiatives.

Curriculum concerns

The curriculum is the fundamental means through which the objectives of futures education are transmitted. It is the basis on which knowledge, skills and attitudes are introduced, engaged with and built so as to provide children with the conceptual framework necessary to understand the future and reflect on its implications for the present. The concept of curriculum renewal accordingly informs the objectives of all futures educators. Futures educators emphasise the importance of an integrated curriculum, seeking to move beyond the discrete, discipline-oriented system of traditional curricula to a broader, interdisciplinary approach (Unesco 1987: 10; Benjamin 1989: 10). This approach to curriculum construction has the advantage of establishing links between different aspects of the curriculum and of recognising the complex range of factors influencing each element of the curriculum. The traditional educational discipline, which commonly claims possession of a single, unitary meaning by excluding divergent or opposing methodologies, is countered in this model by a more open-ended set of teaching and learning strategies. The emphasis in the futures-based curriculum is not so much on learning facts as on the process of learning how to learn, nor so much on acquiring absolute knowledge as on the development of varying skills and attitudes towards learning (Postman and Weingartner 1969: 172; Van Avery 1979: 10).

The more open-ended curriculum prepares students well for adulthood since it reflects more accurately the dynamism and diversity which characterises contemporary society and the open-endedness of the future. It is also more flexible and responsive to the continuing learning processes of individuals (Sachs 1990: 17). The futures-oriented curriculum would allow many points of entry for students' differing needs and interests and would adopt appropriately varied methods of instruction and options of instructional objectives (Glaser 1975: 131; Kauffman 1980: 47).

Collaboration and participation

This principle of flexibility provides students with a heightened awareness of the importance of their own roles in shaping the curriculum. A flexible curriculum would enable students to perceive the extent to which learning grows out of a process of collaboration between students and the educator. Students would, in this manner, be encouraged to view themselves as pro-active and in control of setting the agenda for the curriculum. This approach has the potential to render the curriculum more personally meaningful to the students (Australian Curriculum Studies Association 1993: 43; Cumming 1994: 42). Students engage more readily with a curriculum that embraces their interests and concerns (Wilson and Wyn 1987: 119).

The students' sense of control of the curriculum would also reinforce their understanding of one of the key principles of futures studies: that individuals should develop skills to enable them actively to control their destinies rather than passively to accept them (Slaughter 1985: 5). This emphasis, futures educators would argue, demonstrates the degree to which the objectives of futures education are already consonant with the central principles of traditional educational approaches. The futures-oriented curriculum shares with the traditional curriculum the fundamental goal of providing students with the means to exercise participation and choice in their present and future lives (Beare, cited in Crawford 1992: 81). The main distinction between the traditional curriculum and the futures-oriented curriculum, in this respect, is one of emphasis. The futures studies curriculum explicitly situates choice and active participation more fully at the forefront of its objectives.

Sense of self and critical thinking

The previous discussion has highlighted the emphasis in futures education on the development of a strong self-concept. An active, participatory approach to education encourages this by placing the individual's sense of self at the forefront of change. For Draper Kauffman and Eleanora Masini, the cultivation of a sense of self is particularly important for contemporary education. A strong self-concept can constitute an internal anchor for individuals seeking to negotiate a dynamic and changing world (Kauffman 1980: 45; Masini 1982: 7). It also encourages the development of their sense of self-motivation so that they can assume responsibility for propelling themselves through life (Barnes 1978: 123).

The combination of flexibility and self-motivation in the futures-oriented curriculum also encourages students to consider, more broadly, ways in which they can counter the narrowly defined roles which are often assigned to them by society with new roles and concepts (Combs 1981: 370; Slaughter 1994: 41). The futures-oriented curriculum would facilitate the development of the students' ability to renew their thinking by continually reassessing and, where necessary, modifying their understanding of concepts against their changing experiences. Students would, in this manner, be encouraged to accept and enjoy the challenge of living with ambiguities and differing alternatives rather than with a closed sense of meaning which is achieved only through a reductive denial of the richness of experience (Van Avery, 1980: 442).

Futures educators are careful, at the same time, not to adopt an inherently relativist approach to education. The literature sometimes includes reference to the condition of postmodernity, and futures educators would certainly share the concerns of these commentators to reveal the basis of knowledge in ideology and power relations. But the vast majority of futures educators do not seek to construct curricula based around the anti-humanist critiques of much post-structuralist critical theory (Doll 1989: 243–53; Slaughter 1989a: 255–70). Futures education is, instead, characterised by a consistently strong ethical and philosophical orientation which seeks to instil in students a sense of their place in what has been described recently as 'a truly global web of social and ecological relationships' (Slaughter 1994: 14–15).

This philosophical orientation accords with the fundamental objective of futures studies to facilitate students' recognition of their connections with the outside world of culture, society and the environment. The holistic, global perspective results in an emphasis on students developing qualities of respect and tolerance of others, as well as empathy, an appreciation of diversity and difference, and a strong sense of justice and equality (Allen and Plante 1980: 115; Combs 1981: 372; Beare, 1984: 130; Griffin 1985: 23). These principles are also recognised in Article 29 of the Convention on the Rights of the Child in its emphasis on individual and cultural diversity and mutually tolerant citizenship in a free society.

The development of these attitudes results in an emphasis on celebrating the differing knowledge and skills brought by children into educational settings. These include language, cultural heritage and life experiences, as well as differing skills, abilities, interests and outlooks. To recognise these features by making them visible in the curriculum creates the additional benefit of assisting children and their families to feel that they have something distinctive and valuable to contribute to the educational setting. The importance of ensuring that children of ethnic, religious, linguistic minorities or indigenous origins have opportunities to enjoy their culture, to practise or profess their religion and to use their language with others is also highlighted in Article 30 of the Convention of the Rights of the Child.

The emphasis on students reflecting on issues beyond their immediate concerns also results in the frequently established link between futures education and environmental awareness, a connection which is evident, for example, in the series of publications on futures education sponsored by the World Wide Fund for Nature (Joicey 1986; Lorenzo 1986; Greig *et al.* 1987; Fountain 1990; Smart 1991). In an educational setting, this emphasis seeks to enhance students' awareness of the extent to which each forms part of a broader, interconnected network of relationships, an understanding which, as we have seen, was generally absent from the previously cited attitudes of young people to the future. The nurturing of understanding and respect for nature has the added benefit of assisting children to feel a sense of being in touch with the world and, through this, to have some level of control over it. By planning for the environment and seeing an outcome, children can begin to experience that their ideas can be put into action and can have positive benefits for themselves and others.

There is an idealism inherent in much of this thinking, and futures educators occasionally refer directly to the Utopian tradition from which they derive some of their fundamental perspectives (Hicks 1991b: 634). But futures educators in most instances are careful to temper the idealism of their beliefs with an equally strong emphasis on sustained critical thinking and social engagement. For Slaughter, the process of questioning the taken-for-granted truths of society, of 'probing beneath the surface' of accepted norms and conventions, constitutes one of the key lessons of futures education. An enterprise of this kind, he suggests, will not result in a deconstruction of the frameworks of meaning, but will rather heighten the quality of meaning that students can derive from the curriculum (Slaughter 1991b: 34).

This emphasis on critical thinking lies behind the frequent reference in futures educational studies to the development of such thinking skills as flexibility, curiosity, inventiveness, creativity, imagination and the ability to deal with surprise, conflict and a lack of resolution (Goodlad 1973: 220; Tinkler 1987: 4). The reassessment and redefinition of fundamental meanings and assumptions involved in critical thinking will further assist students to view themselves as creators of change, rather than as passive recipients of the future, and to contemplate a range of options for the future rather than a fixed, singular ideal (Beare and Slaughter 1993: 114–15).

Futures education is thus concerned with understanding the processes of change and developing the ability within individuals to control and direct their futures. Educational studies of this kind encourage individuals not to fear change but to feel that they can manipulate and influence events in the future. They also stress individuals' links with the outside world so that they can come to recognise the extent to which they are bound together as individuals forming a common future. The relevance of the development of these skills for individuals in the present is immediately obvious. The development of these skills is of fundamental significance on the deepest and most pervasive level of human development as they encourage a positive self-concept and a sense of connectedness with the outside world.

Educational initiatives with futures-oriented components

A number of recent initiatives can be cited to illustrate some of the ways in which these principles have been applied in educational settings. Ray Lorenzo's *Immaginiamo il futuro* project (*Let's Shape the Future*) was sponsored by the World Wildlife Fund (Lorenzo and Lepore 1990). In this project, primary and secondary school children from around Italy were asked to consider ways in which they could improve their local environments. Modifications to the environment were devised by means of designs, created in a variety of media, which were then submitted to a jury of teachers, environmentalists, futures researchers and young people before being taken to the towns' mayors for discussion and, in some instances, implementation. The project also involved the distribution of a questionnaire which asked children to outline their ideas, fears and wishes concerning the future and environmental issues. Lorenzo disseminated the results of these in seminars offered at the regional, local and national levels (Lorenzo 1989: 4).

The project put into practice all the previously discussed principles of futures education. Its interdisciplinary nature was highlighted by the manner in which it encouraged students to consider the many factors involved in planning successful living spaces, be they environmental, social or aesthetic. It was flexible and open-ended, exploring a range of options for future change rather than a narrowly defined, unitary model of what the future will be like. It was driven by the students' own agendas for change, thus encouraging them to feel pro-active and in control of an educational initiative of direct relevance to their daily lives. Its sense of personal relevance was combined with an equally strong emphasis on the ways in which the students' own concerns were mediated by broader social, political, historical and environmental concerns. By considering their links within the broader environment, the children were also encouraged to move beyond their traditionally defined roles of subordination to their elders. The latter stages of the project enabled them to participate in the power structures to which they were normally denied access, thus opening up a political dimension which Lorenzo understands to be of particular significance to the *Immaginiamo il futuro* project.

The project also highlighted the importance of furthering social and cultural agendas through the medium of creativity and critical thinking. The emphasis on creating images of the future accords with the previously discussed stress in futures education on the use of imagery as a means of enlarging and enriching the individual's sense of the future (Beare and Slaughter 1993: 142–3). The outcomes of this approach are evident in the following children's statements about the future:

> In the future I imagine flying objects … to free the roads. And many suns. Yes three suns. So the day will never end. And many plants too, and we will be able to swim because in every corner there will be a small lake.
>
> (Massimiliano, ten years, cited in Lorenzo 1989: 1)

> I imagine that after many years trees start to grow again and they will be so high that they will touch the sky. And we will climb them to give a look around from their tops. To see how the Earth looks like from the sky.
>
> (Joseph, eleven years, cited in Lorenzo 1989: 1)

By opening their minds to the possibilities of imagination, the children interviewed by Lorenzo set themselves radically apart from the previously discussed young people's commentaries with their dystopian stereotypes of the future. Their quotations are characterised, instead, by a freedom to think laterally and creatively around the problems involved with the future as a means of solving them.

The value of the process of imagining possibilities for the future has also been recognised by the Associazione L'Età Verde (Association of the Green Age) which forms part of the activities of the Italian Futures Organisation, the Club of Rome (Associazione L'Età Verde 1978). Each year L'Età Verde sponsors children aged between six and sixteen years in a number of Italian schools to research topics of concern related to their future environment. The children are encouraged to formulate a range of strategies to address the issues, many of which take the form of visual images. The projects are then displayed to the public and a meeting is held to discuss them. L'Età Verde is directly comparable, in its principal objectives, to Lorenzo's *Immaginiamo il futuro*. It also encourages children to harness creativity and imagination in order to develop a sense of control over the future and to engage critically and inventively with the problems and power structures created by adults. The projects place children first, encouraging them to recognise their common links with a diverse group of individuals, all of whom are there in order to support and recognise their ideas and contributions.

The initiators of these projects chose to operate independently of traditional school curricula. David Hicks, on the other hand, has centred his exploration of futures-oriented concepts on subjects taught in conventional school curricula. Hicks' work provides a useful demonstration of how skills, attitudes and knowledge can be addressed across the curriculum. His project, *Exploring Alternative Futures*, which was also sponsored by the World Wide Fund for Nature, sought to examine how futures-based objectives and activities could be achieved within the framework of the English National Curriculum. The project was aimed at children aged nine to fourteen attending primary and secondary schools. Hicks' objectives were framed around three main questions: Where are we now? Where do we want to go? and How do we get there? As with the previously discussed projects, Hicks also sought to utilise the skills of visualising alternatives and critical thinking as a means towards bringing into actuality the students' choices for the future (Hicks 1991a, 1994).

Hicks' initiative demonstrates how the objectives of futures education can be applied in different subjects across the curriculum. Another initiative of this kind was the 1986–8 *Bicentennial Futures Project*, which was developed by the Australian Bicentennial Authority and the Commission for the Future during a time of national reflection as the country prepared itself for the 200-year anniversary of white settlement in Australia. This project sought to advance futures thinking across the educational spectrum (Tickell 1987: 17–19, 1989: 70–3). It involved the implementation in twelve primary and secondary schools from around Australia of a draft set of educational materials which were directed towards encouraging students to analyse their options for the future (Tickell and Peterson 1987: 14). The ideas generated by the programme were discussed in a weekly radio broadcast and in young people's discussion groups. As with L'Età Verde and *Immaginiamo il futuro*, the project emphasised the use of children's images and expressions on the future as a means of understanding and realising desires for future experiences (Ryan 1986: 11).

The Bicentennial Futures Project constituted a worthwhile initial step towards a greater understanding of futures issues during a year in which Australians reflected on the past with a mind towards their aspirations for the future. It was ultimately unsuccessful, however, in sustaining and fully implementing its programme. A projected resource package of curriculum ideas was formulated but never distributed to schools (Crunden *et al.* 1989). Plans for a national exhibition of children's images of the future were likewise unsuccessful. The project foundered, moreover, on the difficulties involved in incorporating futures issues into the established school curriculum. The difficulties involved in the implementation of this project thus further signal the need for a prolonged examination of the application of futures issues in established educational curricula. The Bicentennial Futures Project was, nonetheless, important in establishing the groundwork for further educational initiatives in Australia. Seven years after its inception, a review of the school curriculum sponsored by the Queensland state government not only recognised the importance of providing young people with the means of analysing their attitudes to the future, but also recommended 'that every syllabus in every subject should have a futures perspective, tackling new timely topics and crucial current social issues' ('Shaping the Future: The Wiltshire Report on the Queensland School Curriculum', 1994).

Conclusion

These examples offer a glimpse into a vital and emerging field of educational practice and research. They help to emphasise the global nature of futures education and to highlight the need which still exists for the development of a coordinated network of educational bodies, non-government organisations and individuals who might join together in order to share ideas, evaluate initiatives and benefit from each other's perspectives. They should also have underscored, for the purposes of the present study, the extent to which futures educators have hitherto directed most of their attention to the task of futures-oriented education in tertiary, secondary and primary educational contexts. Futures education, with only a very few exceptions, has not reached early childhood education. The aims of education, however, need constantly to be related back to the broader issue of the developmental differences of children as they progress through the educational system. While the broad aims of an educational mission will remain intact, the ways in which educators seek to achieve those aims and the timing of when educational content is introduced to children will differ. Any discussion concerning how best to impart in children the knowledge, skills, outlooks and insights necessary to function effectively in the present and future should therefore carefully consider how these concerns can be applied to the developing skills, abilities, outlooks, interests and needs of the children at differing stages of their development.

A match between the objectives of futures education and the developmental requirements of pre-school children is not as difficult to achieve or as alien to the patterns of early childhood development as it might initially appear. Four- and five-year-olds are, after all, much less ego-centric than one- and two-year-olds. They have more experiences to draw on when they come into contact with new ideas, experiences and individuals. They have a better chance of making sense of their world and more opportunity, due to increased mobility, to explore and expand the parameters of their world.

Their personal focus on issues is accordingly combined with a developing sense of the outside world which will increase over the coming years. Four- and five-year-old children are thus already attempting the challenging task of reconciling their personal understandings with broader and more abstract frameworks. In this way, they remain well placed to engage with the social and philosophical objectives of futures studies articulated above.

Chapter 5

Futures studies and early childhood education

On a fundamental level, early childhood education constitutes a highly appropriate forum for the exploration of futures issues. Its positioning at the commencement of formal education provides it with the critical role of introducing children to learning concepts and principles that will remain with them throughout their formal education. Early childhood professionals are thus faced with the challenge of laying the philosophical foundations necessary for the acquisition of skills, abilities and attitudes that will enable the young children in their charge to negotiate successfully the education system as a whole.

There can also be no doubting the potential effectiveness of pre-school education as the medium for the transmission of the broad cultural and social concerns with which futures studies seek to engage. Over half a million children attend Australian early childhood programmes (McLennan 1996: 239–41). The pattern of increasing full-time parent employment ensures that this number can only increase. It has been recently estimated that some children may spend up to 12,500 hours in childcare before entering school (National Childcare Accreditation Council 1993: foreword). Early childhood professionals thus need to give consideration to their considerable influence upon children and their corresponding responsibility to best meet the future needs of the young children in their care. In order to achieve this, they need to address how they can provide children with the skills and outlooks required to devise positive frameworks of understanding for the future and to cope as adults in the fluid and dynamic contemporary society. In this way they can act as positive advocates for the young children in their charge.

It might be argued, in the first instance, that it would be unrealistic to apply the long-term perspective of futures education to the essentially short-term objectives of early childhood. Such an argument would seriously underestimate both the principles of early childhood education and the significance of the early childhood curriculum. It has already been noted that early childhood professionals share with the proponents of futures studies an understanding of education as the means for enhancing long-term development (Woodhead 1985; Lee *et al.* 1990; Sroufe *et al.* 1990; Wasik *et al.* 1990; Zigler and Muenchow 1992; Schweinhart 1993). The formulation of long- and short-term learning objectives in the early childhood curriculum is fundamentally directed towards fostering future development. By addressing curriculum concerns and content in terms of the long-term needs and skills of children, early childhood professionals seek to lay the foundations for lifelong learning.

Long-term objectives in early childhood education

The work of the High/Scope Educational Research Foundation during the 1960s, provides a tangible example of the positive long-term influence that a sensitively planned pre-school programme can have on young children's development (Halliwell 1990: 48). Longitudinal studies have established that the children attending Head Start programmes were better equipped with long-term developmental skills than children from comparable backgrounds (Woodhead 1985: 134–5). The Head Start programme shared with the principles of futures education the aspiration to look beyond the traditionally narrow developmental concerns of conventional curricula. As with futures education, the Head Start programme sought to engage meaningfully with the broader social issues which negatively effect growth and development. Part of the programme's success in achieving these aims lay in its emphasis upon another key principle of futures education, that of encouraging students to renew their connections with the wider social contexts with which they engage. Woodhead has noted of the project that:

> the positive experience of pre-school triggered a virtuous cycle of changes not only in the children, but in their relationship to their family and school, and in turn to their wider social context in which they were gaining competence.
>
> (Woodhead 1985: 230)

This is, or should be, a particularly important emphasis in early childhood education since, in many instances, early childhood centres constitute the first social institutions with which young children come into contact. In contradistinction to the rhetoric of much educational research and policy-making, the High/Scope programme seriously addressed its stated aim to foster lifelong learning. It thus stands as an important model for the application of the long-term goals of futures studies in early childhood education.

Early childhood education shares a number of other principles with futures studies. As with futures studies, early childhood educational theorists stress the multidimensionality of growth and development. Theorists have long emphasised the extent to which early childhood development occurs as a result of the interaction of a complex range of psychological, sexual, physical, sociological and other factors. In order to understand the full richness of the integrated model of development, early childhood theorists have, in common with the proponents of futures studies, adopted an interdisciplinary approach, blending the insights of education with those of psychology, philosophy, sociology, critical theory and political science (National Association for the Education of Young Children 1991: 23).

Piaget and Vygotsky have also acknowledged the importance of the dynamic interaction of past, present and future learnings in child growth and development (Piaget 1951: 1–4; Vygotsky 1978: 22). This understanding emphasises the importance of individuals revisiting past learnings in order to make sense of the present and to project their new understandings into the future. Viewed from this perspective, children's thinking is seen as constantly evolving, as thought processes are continuously reassessed and modified in the light of new information. Their concentration on the flexibility of thought processes accords with the stress in futures studies on flexibility as a fundamental means of dealing with diversity and change. Bronfenbrenner's ecological model recognises the connections between these evolving growth patterns and the wider social contexts with which children engage (Bronfenbrenner 1979). His comments on the reciprocal links between the significant environments in children's lives and the manner in which children form part of an interconnected network of social factors accord well with the previously discussed social and cultural orientation of futures studies.

These theories provide the conceptual underpinnings to many of the concerns dealt with in the formulation of early childhood curricula. The many divergences involved in the study of early childhood developmental theory mean, nonetheless, that the early childhood professional is faced with the challenge of bringing together certain key concepts in order to achieve a view of development which is holistic yet integrative and internally consistent (Mialarat 1976: 35). Futures studies offers a cogent and flexible framework with which to respond to this challenge.

Futures studies researchers, early childhood professionals and futures education

A number of futures studies researchers and early childhood professionals have recognised in general terms the relevance of futures studies for early childhood. Futures studies researchers frequently highlight the fact that it is children, rather than adults, who will create the world of the future, with some arguing from this the need for a greater attention to futures studies in early childhood education (Shane and Shane 1974: 182; Masini 1986a: 7). Troutman and Palombo have argued from this that the developmental emphasis of the early childhood educational curriculum renders it a highly appropriate context for the application of futures concerns (Troutman and Palombo 1983: 49). A number of futures researchers have also stressed the importance of early childhood education as a forum for laying the foundations for future growth and lifelong learning (Allen and Plante 1980: 116; Pierce 1980: 68–70; Masini 1981: 3; Benjamin 1989: 11). Ford has noted, in this context, the need to coordinate a futures-focused curriculum at the early childhood level of education with similar initiatives at later levels of education. If this were achieved, she argues, futures studies could form an effective counter-agent to the fragmentation of learning which frequently occurs in conventional educational curricula (Ford 1980: 6–7).

Several futures studies researchers have highlighted the degree to which young children already possess some of the attitudes which futures studies seeks to encourage. Nicholson and Masini have noted the liveliness and unpredictability of young children, as well as their ability to question, create, cooperate and intuit (Nicholson 1979: 270; Masini nd: 81–4). Lorenzo has stressed children's powers of imagination, creativity and their interest in fantasy (Lorenzo 1989: 2). He observes that these qualities allow children to explore possibilities and options for the future which adults frequently neglect. He also points out that children's nimbleness, quick-wittedness and natural inclination to treat the world as a laboratory provide them with a real insight into humanity's potential to create alternative worlds. These are all qualities which adults should seek to rediscover and which young children begin to lose all too soon in their experience of primary and secondary education.

Several authors have focused on the futures-oriented skills, attitudes and wider learnings that young children need to acquire during the early years of education. The skills most commonly stressed in this regard are adaptability, imagination and fantasy (Shane and Shane 1974: 187–93; Pierce 1980: 68–70; Toda 1993: 364). Other skills and outlooks which have been noted include altruism, sensitivity towards others, conflict resolution and decision-making (Pierce 1980: 68–9). Harold and June Shane have emphasised the importance of introducing children to the nature of change and choice for future alternatives. They also note the desirability of encouraging children to develop a strong self-image which can be projected into the future (Shane and Shane 1974: 186–8, 191–2).

Early childhood theorists generally address future-related issues from a somewhat different perspective. Lacking the broader methodological orientation of futures studies, they tend to focus more commonly on the identification of skills which a futures-focused educational programme should address. A number have highlighted the need to provide children with the necessary skills and knowledge for the future, with some noting the need for these skills to be relevant to the dynamic nature of contemporary society (Watts 1987: 9–14; Caldwell 1988: 13–15; Short 1991: 11). Early childhood professionals tend to overlap with futures studies researchers in the kinds of skills which they identify as important in this respect. Ebbeck, among others, has noted that, in order to cope with dynamism and change, children need to develop resilience, empathy and adaptability, an interest in creativity and in other cultures, and skills in communication, problem-solving and lateral thinking (Ebbeck 1983: 9–12; Watts 1987: 4–12; Caldwell 1988: 13–15; Clyde 1984: 8; Hildebrand 1991b: 64–65). Almy has noted that early childhood professionals will need to possess these skills and attitudes themselves, if they intend to encourage their development in young children (M. Almy, *The Early Childhood Educator at Work*, 1975, cited in Saracho and Spodek 1993: 10). The ability of early childhood professionals to consider their feelings towards the future and attitudes towards their roles in shaping the future is fundamental to the effective translation of these skills into early childhood curriculum frameworks and will be returned to in the final chapter of this study.

A smaller number of commentators have related the concerns of futures studies to the wider issues of curriculum construction and the role of early childhood education in contemporary society. Clyde has recognised the relevance of futures studies to the task of creating early childhood curricula which are fully accountable to the changing needs of their clientele (Clyde 1984: 4). Watts, Power and Balson have, in like manner, emphasised that futures-related issues can assist early childhood professionals to develop curricula which remain educationally relevant to the changing demands of contemporary society and which do not fall into the trap of replicating outmoded social and cultural stereotypes (Balson 1981: 24–8; Watts 1987: 9–10; Power 1993: 53–9). Silin stresses the importance of early childhood professionals understanding the political nature of teaching and of viewing the curriculum against the 'larger societal processes that shape and are shaped by it' (Silin 1988: 126). The *Te Whariki* document (Ritchie 1996) also acknowledges the political nature of the early childhood curriculum. While an early childhood curriculum will be based in the 'social and political reality', of the early childhood community, it can also act as a powerful instrument through which to overcome the socially and politically embedded inequality and racism (Lubeck 1994: 18; Ritchie 1996: 32) which often remain unchallenged (and are thus at least tacitly reinforced) in traditional early childhood curricula (Cannella 1997: 1–2).

Few commentators have sought to engage with the broad social and cultural issues dealt with in futures studies. Halliwell has noted the need for professionals to understand and address the wider social contexts in which they work (Halliwell 1990: 50). She notes the limitations inherent in the common tendency among professionals to concentrate too narrowly on the child's immediate environment (Halliwell 1992b: 130). Her comments have been echoed by Morris who has also stressed the responsibility of early childhood professionals to adopt a global dimension to their educational outlook (Morris 1991: 89–92). Keliher has noted the importance of adopting creative learning strategies if such objectives are to be realised in early childhood curricula (Keliher 1986: 42–4).

These studies notwithstanding, it should nonetheless be recognised that very few professionals have addressed the implications involved in translating futures studies concerns into curriculum construction. This constitutes a significant limitation in the study conducted in the area thus far. It is, after all, a relatively easy task to articulate general ideals for learning. It is much more difficult to identify the specific vision and strategies necessary for achieving these aims in operative curricula. This approach has also been lacking in the work of futures researchers, mainly because the outlook of their discipline is not so commonly directed towards the practical implementation of educational curricula. This task is made more difficult in early childhood education by the fact that futures studies has not yet directed its attention to the field. Futures studies was initially directed towards tertiary and secondary education and thereafter to an examination of its relevance to primary education. It has not, as a whole, taken on the task of addressing early childhood education.

This limitation in the field is further exacerbated by the fact that futures studies is not, at present, being taught systematically at the level of pre-service training. As a result, early childhood professionals remain largely unaware of the relevance of futures studies to curriculum formulation. The lack of research and writing in this area has tended to compound the problem, resulting in the production of very little accessible information on the topic. A programme of research, teacher training, in-service training and publications will need to be developed in order to offer support to early childhood professionals in this respect. These challenges should not be perceived as insurmountable obstacles to the development of futures-focused curricula in early childhood. We have already seen the many principles that are shared by futures studies and curriculum theory and practice in early childhood education. These parallels become even clearer when we examine more closely the principles and practices involved in the construction of early childhood curricula.

Futures studies and early childhood curriculum formulation

> No work is more fundamentally future-oriented than curriculum development; its purpose, after all is to prepare the next generation for the coming age.
>
> (Noyce 1986: foreword)

The fundamental purpose of curriculum construction is to define the parameters in which future development will be fostered. As such, it should constitute the main focus of any attempt to achieve a futures-orientation in education. It is through the curriculum that knowledge and attitudes are imparted, skills are refined, and time and direction are offered to children in a manner which encourages them to engage actively with the issues and concepts addressed by the professional.

The early childhood curriculum is particularly well suited to incorporate a futures studies framework since early childhood professionals are not required to teach a set syllabus, as are their colleagues in primary and secondary education. They thus have the scope to construct curricula with a greater sense of freedom and flexibility and responsiveness to the complexity of child growth and development than the prescribed curricula of primary and secondary educational settings.

Curriculum construction at the early childhood level of education is, moreover, an inherently futures-oriented process. It combines the practical with the theoretical in a manner which is directly commensurate with futures issues. The formulation of the early childhood curriculum involves the translation of theoretical tenets into a series of practical applications. Early childhood professionals translate their broad philosophy or vision into a set of values which are refined into both general and specific objectives. This process is then refined further into the practical implementation of individual learning experiences within the time and space of the programme session.

This process, it should be stressed, is not primarily aimed towards the achievement of specific, easily definable outcomes such as are promoted by the behaviourist school of developmental theory. As Clark has pointed out, the behavioural model limits itself through its definition of objectives as a series of quantifiable terminal behaviours. This suggests a passivity on the part of the learner and involves the assumption that knowledge is finite and can be somehow measured as a series of factual building blocks (Clark 1988: 53). Early childhood professionals have the potential to construct the curriculum as a series of dynamic and open-ended objectives which are continuously modified to suit the changing needs and interests of the children over time and into the future. Early childhood practitioners are accordingly concerned with the total child, rather than with dissecting development and growth into easily observable components. They recognise child growth and development as complex processes and that the different aspects of a child's being are interconnected and will influence one another (Arthur et al. 1996: 76). This holistic orientation towards curriculum construction requires them to take into consideration the interrelations between the many differing aspects of child growth, be they physical, emotional, psychological, spiritual, cultural, intellectual or social. The early childhood professional has a corresponding autonomy to create a curriculum which remains responsive to the complexity of child growth and development.

The principle of active learning is also commensurate with the objectives of futures studies. Curriculum planning has always incorporated an emphasis upon providing time, space and direction for the manipulation of learning materials. This approach accords with the stress in futures studies on assisting individuals to feel in control of the environment by understanding their place within it. The concepts of change and adaptation are also central to the objectives of the early childhood curriculum. Early childhood professionals focus on the developing thought processes, skills and abilities of individual children. They modify the curriculum constantly in order to render it responsive to the changing developmental needs of each child, thus affording due recognition to the importance of individualised learning which has long been a central premise of early childhood curriculum construction. By adopting this approach to education, early childhood professionals signal their commitment to valuing the need for children to set their own agendas for change, an objective which they share with the proponents of futures studies.

An emphasis on children as individuals will also give rise to a learning environment that offers 'equitable opportunities for learning irrespective of gender, disability, age, ethnicity or background', and one that will 'work to ensure that young children are not discriminated against on the basis of gender, age, race, religion, language, ability, culture or national origin' (Australian Early Childhood Association 1991: 4; Ministry of Education 1996: 64). By acknowledging and respecting individual children and the diversity that they bring to the curriculum as a whole, early childhood professionals convey to children a strong message concerning their worth in the programme. A strong self-concept is the means through which children develop a sense of security in the learning environment as well as the agency to develop meaningful relationships with others. In this way, respect for individual children and for their right to feel acknowledged and empowered through the curriculum can be viewed as the cornerstone of the early childhood curriculum.

The process of planning for the individual in the curriculum will also bring the early childhood professional into contact with a number of other principles of futures studies. Over the course of the year, the early childhood professional observes the different ways in which each child engages with the environment in order to gain meaning from it. These observations provide important insights into the position of each child in the broader pattern of developmental norms. They form the basis of an individually tailored programme of experiences which is designed in order to acknowledge, reinforce and extend the child's skills, life experiences and understandings. Early childhood curricula are thus founded on a detailed awareness and recognition of the dynamism and complexity of child growth. Early childhood professionals share with the proponents of futures studies, in this respect, an aspiration to move beyond the traditional, unitary model of teaching. They recognise the extent to which each early childhood curriculum is comprised of a number of interconnected, yet inherently flexible, educational programmes which operate concurrently.

The ability of early childhood professionals to remain responsive to the complexity and diversity of child growth is aided by the flexibility of their methods of evaluating the children's development. The constant modification of the curriculum to best meet the objectives set for each child's development grows out of a continuous process of observation and evaluation of children's activities. This information is traditionally compiled from profiles for each child attending the programme. The system of child profiles frees the professional from the restrictions imposed on many primary and secondary school teachers. Rather than having to fit the child to a pre-set programme, the early childhood professional has the flexibility to construct the programme around the differing needs of each individual child. The information contained in the child profile reflects this diversity. It may take the form of anecdotal pieces of information, running records of a child's interaction, samples of language and/or art work, thus affording within the very methods of curriculum construction due recognition of the kaleidoscopic nature of child growth and learning.

This approach to education provides the professional and the children with a sense of shared ownership of the curriculum. By incorporating within the learning environment a number of diverse, yet interconnecting learning experiences, the professional encourages the children to develop a sense of independence and freedom to exercise choice and to explore alternative learning experiences. The responsiveness of the curriculum to differing needs and interests enables children to begin to perceive that their goals are accessible and that their ideas can be realised. At a vital stage of their early development, children are to be given an understanding of the extent to which their ideas are valued and can be put into action.

An orientation of this kind significantly empowers children in the process of learning. As early childhood professionals act to support and extend individual children's skills, abilities, interests, life experiences, insights, values and future knowledge, they will render the early childhood curriculum open to the children and allow them the scope to co-determine its nature and content. Children will now recognise their control over a curriculum which has become personally meaningful to them in a manner which is in complete accordance with the principles of futures education. Through the collaborative process, the child gains a sense of being valued and recognised as an autonomous and active participant and decision-maker within the early childhood environment. Children who come into contact with this form of curriculum will be encouraged not to fear change but, rather, to feel in control of the processes of change and adaptation. This dynamic understanding of the concepts of change and adaptation, once again, shares much in common with the objectives of futures studies. A child-initiated curriculum acknowledges children as active agents, capable of expressing, determining and acting upon what interests and motivates them. It also provides children with the freedom to 'continue learning with an enhanced sense of self-worth, identity, confidence and enjoyment; contribute their own special strengths and interests, learn useful and appropriate ways to find out what they want to know [and] understand their individual ways of learning and being creative' (Ministry of Education 1996: 40).

Of equal importance is the extent to which this multi-faceted, participatory model of education encourages children to recognise the broader social dimension to each individualised learning experience. Children are encouraged within this framework to recognise the manner in which the projection and realisation of ideas within a learning environment involves them in sharing and negotiating those ideas with others. The curriculum functions, in this respect, as a combination of individually and socially oriented learnings. The relative value of each factor in the combination of elements will vary constantly according to the differing needs and developmental levels of each individual involved. It is also contingent upon the input of the adult professional who, as Vygotsky and Bruner have stressed, provides a social meaning and purpose to the learnings undertaken by the children (Fleer 1992: 142).

The links forged between children in the learning environment thus allow the early childhood curriculum to function as a microcosm of the broader social contexts with which the children will engage throughout their lives. The children's interaction with the social environment of the early childhood centre acts both to validate their understanding of the world and also to provide them with the opportunity to reflect this broader social experience back into the personalised agenda for development which is equally to be nurtured and extended by the professional. The sensitively maintained balance between the personal and social contexts of the early childhood curriculum thus, once again, aligns early childhood education with the central objective of futures education: to provide a forum for individuals to recognise their links with the outside world of culture, society and the environment.

An awareness of this aspect of the curriculum also requires that the professional establish connections between the learning environment and the many other environments with which the child engages. The role of parents and caregivers in the child's education should, for example, constitute a further important consideration in curriculum design. Parents and caregivers are the child's primary agents for education and, as such, should be drawn upon as significant sources of information about their children. Conversely, early childhood professionals can offer parents and caregivers important perspectives on their child's development. The recognition between parents and professionals that they both share complementary goals, gives rise to a sense of partnership (Henry 1996: 15; Rodd 1998: 163). A central understanding underlying the partnership approach is 'the common goal of caring for and educating a child or children' which is to be based on an attitude of mutual respect and understanding (Hughes and MacNaughton 1999: 221).

By sharing information, early childhood professionals and parents can collaborate in order to ensure that the curriculum best accommodates the differing needs of each child. Part of the importance of the development of positive parent–professional relationships lies in the manner in which it provides a means of demonstrating to children the connections between the different aspects of their lives (Keliher 1986: 42–4). This approach has the additional benefit of enabling parents and professionals to act as resources for each other so that links and continuities can be built between the child's experiences in the early childhood programme and in the home environment. It further allows the professional to build into the curriculum a fuller consideration of those family, cultural and community considerations which equally influence a child's development. In so doing, the professional recognises the importance of the principles of empathy for others and appreciation of social and cultural diversity which, we have seen, are commonly stressed in futures studies. It also sets up the opportunity of a community of inquiry in which the children's families and early childhood professionals co-construct knowledge by actively joining together to discuss, debate, question, hypothesise and negotiate knowledge and in so doing create a meaningful learning environment for the children.

Much of the work of early childhood professionals is thus already in close accord with the objectives of futures studies. As a result, a futures-focused curriculum should not involve anything radically new or not already in keeping with the professional's fundamental objective: to remain responsive to the developmental needs of the children. The early childhood curriculum has the potential to act as a nexus between the practical and the theoretical dimensions of futures issues. Both the curriculum and futures studies can provide a reference point for each other so that the range of exploration remains neither too remote nor too limited in scope.

Chapter 6

Applying futures concerns to the early childhood curriculum

The previous discussion has underlined the importance to the curriculum of a wide range of socially and personally oriented futures concerns. It has established the appropriateness of the early childhood curriculum for the exploration of these issues. Applying these concerns in the early childhood curriculum need not involve the early childhood professional in any radically new philosophical and educational frameworks. Rather, it provides a means of extending and re-articulating existing developmental objectives from the vantage point of new perspectives. The discussion of four- and five-year-old children's views on the future also demonstrated their readiness to engage with some of the key concepts of futures studies. The young children of the interviews were seen already to possess many of the positive attitudes towards time and the future which futures studies researchers seek to re-instil in adults and older children. But while it has been established that the outlook of young children and the nature of the early childhood curriculum share much in common with the emphases of futures studies, the question remains as to how the objectives of a futures-focused curriculum should be defined and then translated into practical learning experiences.

This chapter will draw on the previous discussion as a means of defining the curriculum foci of a futures-oriented curriculum. The open and flexible nature of the early childhood curriculum means that it would be inappropriate to present a fixed, definitive curriculum along these lines. What follows will serve instead to illustrate some of the ways in which these concepts could be applied in the early childhood curriculum. Some of these foci are recognised early childhood principles whose relevance to futures studies will be drawn out. Others, which relate more specifically to the previously discussed principles of futures studies, will be interpreted as complementing and extending upon the pre-existing objectives of the early childhood curriculum.

Curriculum foci for a futures-oriented early childhood curriculum

- *The development of strong self-concepts in the children*
- *For children to develop relationships of trust and security with staff and peers*
- *The development of forward looking perspectives in the children*

The previous chapters have returned repeatedly to young children's strong sense of connectedness to the outside world. Early childhood professionals should seek to capitalise on this sense of confidence by placing a correspondingly strong emphasis in the early childhood programme on the development of a positive self-concept. Self-esteem serves as a fundamentally important developmental factor from the earliest stage of development. It is, in one sense, particularly important in the early childhood setting because it is largely developed in social environments in interactions with others. Research studies have indicated that children aged 3–5 years typically have a high self-esteem which is largely founded on a sense of social acceptance and social competence which has been facilitated by adults and others (Berk 1997: 428–35). It is therefore most important that early childhood professionals consider how individual children perceive themselves within the early childhood community and seek to build on this through the curriculum.

In order to achieve this, they will need to formulate learning experiences which are based on the needs, interests, cultural knowledge, life experiences, abilities, dispositions, desires and skills of the children themselves. Central to the need to accommodate individual children's needs is the understanding that young children 'vary in the rate and timing of their growth and development and in their capacity to learn new things in new places' (Ministry of Education 1996: 20). By acknowledging individuality, the early childhood professional is, by extension, placing value on diversity within the early childhood community. Young children who spend time in early childhood communities with such an emphasis, will be receiving messages concerning their value to others in the early childhood setting. The importance of a strong self-concept cannot be underestimated. It will be a powerful means through which children will develop a sense of security within the learning environment and an agency to develop meaningful relationships with others as well as the ability to develop skills of critical and independent thinking. A sense of security and belonging acts as a strong basis from which a child will actively participate in the learning environment (Malaguzzi 1998: 64). A strong self-concept and correspondingly high self-esteem can be viewed as the foundation from which one's potential can be reached.

The curriculum should also extend its interest in the child's self-esteem by placing a value on the child's cultural and social background as well as his or her own individual personality and interests (Ministry of Education 1996:

40). In so doing, early childhood professionals will be seeking to create an environment that resonates with individual children in meaningful ways by acknowledging and responding to their broader developmental needs as well as to the individual life experiences and diverse social and cultural backgrounds that they bring with them into the early childhood community.

Early childhood professionals also have the potential to extend these approaches into the future by affirming the positive explorations of future identities which were so strongly evident in the comments of the four- and five-year-old children surveyed in Chapter 2. In this respect, they could actively contribute to the task of developing a positive future role image which, Stinchcombe, Singer and others have argued, remains so fundamental to an individual's long-term development (Stinchcombe, cited in Bell and Mau 1971: 33; Singer, cited in Toffler 1974: 19–32).

- *The development of a sense of agency in children*
- *For children to put their ideas into practice*
- *For children to feel active participants in the learning programme and that they can exert some influence over it*

Early childhood professionals who are committed to promoting in children a sense of self-worth will also ensure that children's viewpoints and contributions are acknowledged and acted upon. By acting on children's interests and insights, professionals provide children with the opportunity to become co-collaborators in the process of designing and implementing the curriculum. This requires early childhood professionals to render the curriculum open to the children so as to allow them the scope to co-determine its range and content. A curriculum of this kind will be constantly modified by the educator in order to accommodate the emergent issues and ideas raised by the children's own constantly evolving interests. One of the primary tasks of the early childhood practitioner operating within this kind of curriculum will be to stimulate and guide children's questions as they develop in response to the children's evolving interests and to help give the children the agency to consider and work through each question in turn. In short, a curriculum of this kind has the potential to become primarily an expression of the children themselves.

An emphasis on the emergent and unplanned also provides the early childhood professional the scope to offer the children opportunities to identify and act on what interests them. This approach to curriculum design has been referred to as 'child initiated' and recognises that the child 'has an active role in the initiation of interests, questions, hypotheses and remains a collaborator in the process and form of subsequent inquiry, exploration and creative expression' (Tinworth 1997: 25). A child-initiated curriculum acknowledges that young children are capable of expressing, determining and engaging with what deeply interests and motivates them, and offers them the possibility to take responsibility for their learning. An emphasis of this kind will also promote in young children an image of themselves as autonomous learners. Affirming children for their independent thinking and their individual approach to issues would remain a central focus of the early childhood professional.

- *For children to develop a sense of inquiry*

> We think of a school for young children as an integral living organism, as a place of shared lives and relationships among many adults and very many children. We think of school as a sort of construction in motion, continuously adjusting itself.
>
> (Malaguzzi 1998: 62)

On a collective level, an emphasis on negotiation in the curriculum offers early childhood educators the scope to create a community of ínquiry. According to this model, children, early childhood professionals and parents co-construct knowledge by actively joining together to discuss, debate, question, hypothesise and negotiate knowledge and meaning. A community of inquiry between children, professionals and families also has the advantage of helping to sustain children's interests over extended periods of time (Tinworth 1997: 28). It enables professionals to create direct and relevant links to young children's learning that occurs outside the early childhood curriculum. The early childhood curriculum should become more meaningful to young children when it operates in this way as the links to their experiences outside the early childhood community become visible through the curriculum. An approach of this kind will also emphasise the importance of young children setting their own personalised agendas for change. As children develop a sense of ownership in the curriculum they will grow to recognise that their interests and ideas are valued by the early childhood professionals who will integrate them with their pedagogical objectives. This will promote in the children a growing sense of independence and freedom to exercise choice and explore alternatives.

Early childhood professionals who view children's growth and development in the broader contexts that influence them will also attempt to extend the full range of human developmental concerns – from the spiritual to the cultural and social – and will seek to ensure that the curriculum reflects and is responsive to these concerns. An emphasis will accordingly be placed on the recognition of the broader social, economic, political and cultural forces that impact on children and their families: 'If the goal of education is to inculcate the knowledge and skills that will prepare persons to be successful political and social agents, then it must be informed by the sense of polis that the student will eventually enter' (Silin 1988: 120). Children and families grow and develop within broader social contexts, and are required constantly to negotiate issues concerning their current and long-term needs within these broader contexts. Early childhood professionals need to view their curriculum in terms of whether it is also responsive and sensitive towards these broader concerns. An emphasis of this kind will further foster in children their links to the outside world of culture and society. This can be fostered actively as we shall see in some of the initiatives discussed later in this chapter. It will also reinforce in the children a greater sense of meaning and purpose in environments beyond the early childhood community.

A holistic view of the child will see early childhood professionals placing due recognition on the complex nature of the processes of child growth and development while also acknowledging that different aspects of a child's being are interconnected and will influence each other (Arthur *et al.* 1996: 76). This perspective is complemented by the previously discussed commitment to individuality as early childhood professionals view each child as a complex multi-faceted being. Early childhood professionals will seek to reflect this by offering individual children a rich variety of materials and learning experiences with which they can engage on a number of levels.

•   *For children to engage actively with the learning environment*

Young children learn best when they actively engage with the learning environment (National Association for the Education of Young Children 1992: 21). Active learning provides one of the key means by which young children attempt to make sense of their world (Dockett and Perry 1996: 6). Its implementation in early childhood curricula acknowledges the degree to which young children will develop new 'constructs' by physically, socially, emotionally, intellectually, spiritually, morally and creatively engaging with ideas, materials and equipment. In order to promote this learning in young children Fleet and Clyde stress that early childhood professionals need to ensure that 'learning activities and materials should be concrete, real, and relevant to the lives of young children' (1993: 120). In this way professionals can ensure that the curriculum will offer children an open-ended series of possibilities and choices. As children choose what is of most interest to them they will feel motivated to initiate independent learning and to gain a corresponding sense of confidence in themselves and their abilities as learners.

Viewed from this perspective, the early childhood learning environment has a potential to become a laboratory where young children can act on their sense of wonder, curiosity, interests, needs, ideas and concerns with others. Such an emphasis is also commensurate with a futures-focused curriculum which is concerned with the process of learning rather than with definitive learning outcomes in children. An emphasis on active learning will see early childhood professionals offering children a rich variety of experiences with which they can engage on a number of levels:

The wider the range of possibilities we offer children, the more intense will be their motivations and the richer their experience. We must widen the range of topics and goals, the types of situations we offer and their degree of structure, the kinds and combinations of resources and materials, and the possible interactions with things, peers and adults.

(Malaguzzi 1998: 79)

As children engage with the environment they will further gain a sense of being active members of a lively and evolving community.

- *For children to develop skills of independent thinking and problem-solving*
- *For children to explore conceptual possibilities and make intentional decisions*

Active learning also recognises the extent to which children actively construct knowledge. Developing skills of independent thinking and problem-solving remain central to this approach. A fundamental objective of any futures-oriented curriculum should thus be for the early childhood professional to develop the ability in children to define the parameters of a problem and to identify the questions which need to be answered or steps which need to be implemented in order for that problem or issue to be solved. This approach serves as an important means of furthering an individual's ability to think successfully across the breadth of the educational programme (Lambert 1994: 5). Individuals with a problem-solving approach to thinking will be able to engage critically with ideas and issues which are outside their immediate area of expertise or specialisation. Not all problems can, of course, be solved by this approach. But even where individuals do not possess the specialised skill or data to be able to solve the problem for themselves, they can still go some way towards its resolution or clarification. Problem-solving engenders a flexible approach to thinking since it encourages individuals to establish connections between different concepts and to see the potential for solving problems in new ways. It also enables individuals to feel in control of making decisions about the external factors which influence their lives.

A great deal of experience will remain outside the direct parameters of the early childhood programme. Problem-solving skills which can be transposed to a multitude of broader experiences are thus of the utmost importance for the young child. It is vital that early childhood professionals develop an understanding of the differing levels of knowledge that children possess. Learning environments which are structured to encourage the children's skills of problem-solving will assist them to build a framework of thinking skills that can then be applied to problems as they arise and to use this as a basis for venturing from the familiar to the unknown. In order for this to occur, the learning environment needs to be provided with a broad range of meaningful activities which can be experimented with constantly. Some practical suggestions on how to achieve this emphasis with young children might involve comparing real events with hypothetical events and encouraging children to discuss imaginary situations (Boyer 1997/8: 94). In learning situations, the early childhood professional can assist children to define the parameters of each problem by asking them questions that will encourage their thinking around the different possibilities for its solution.

An example of futures-oriented problem solving in early childhood education is a litter experiment undertaken with a group of children in a kindergarten setting. The experiment arose out of an expressed concern on the children's part about the amount of litter found each day on the kindergarten grounds. After defining the problem, the children and I explored different options for improving the situation. It was eventually decided to erect a sign on the kindergarten fence which read, 'Please do not litter our kindergarten. It could hurt our animals.' We designed the sign, which included the children's images of the animals in the kindergarten, and placed it on the fence. We then monitored the amount of litter found in the playground each day. To the children's delight and pride the amount of litter decreased over time.

While this exercise may appear of minor importance to an adult mind, it was highly significant for the children since it provided them with an avenue through which to engage with many of the key concepts of futures studies. It gave them the opportunity to think creatively and resourcefully, to solve a problem and then to see the results of their intervention in the future. It encouraged them to feel that they could solve a problem by becoming involved in it, thereby exerting a direct influence on their immediate environment and on the safety and welfare of the kindergarten pets. It strengthened their self-concepts and their underlying sense of purpose and motivation, enabling them to make a contribution to the world issue of our threatened environmental resources in a form which was directly relevant to their day-to-day existence.

• *For children to engage with the concept of the future through fantasy and role play*
• *For children to imagine preferred and desired states*

In freely expressing themselves on the topic of the future, the young children discussed earlier in the book vividly demonstrated the extent to which they possess a flexibility of thought that enables them to move through an almost limitless array of different realms and possibilities for the future. A strong sense of the possibilities of fantasy enables these and other young children to explore and master a range of roles within the safe domain and controlling influence of their minds (Boyer 1997/8: 90). We have also seen that play is commonly identified as a fundamentally important conceptual tool.

Slaughter, for example, has underscored its significance, noting that it is only through 'divergent, creative non-standard perception, using fantasy, using imagination, using creativity, that one gets beyond where one is to other sorts of possibilities which are out of the frame ... of the accepted conventional wisdom' (Slaughter, interview with the author 1989). The intellectual empowerment which comes with the exercising of fantasy can assist children to work through issues on a number of different levels. The application of fantasy also has significant social benefits since it is partly through fantasy that children explore concepts of power, control, negotiation and language mastery (Dau 1991: 71–83).

Children can also experience the benefits of fantasy in their interactions with others as part of their play experience. Play has the potential to assist early childhood professionals to observe and evaluate these dynamics as they unfold in their early childhood community and to reflect on whether the early childhood learning environment is offering all children equal opportunity to participate in experiences. A rich variety of open-ended materials and spaces should be available to enable children to explore a number of ideas not only in a group context, but also in more personalised spaces. Mirrors, for example, offer children the opportunity to explore their self-image and different personae.

- *For children to explore a variety of modes of communication, including symbols and visual images*

Early childhood professionals should formulate curricula which reflect the fact that young children are frequently more fluent and articulate in images than they are in language. As evidence of this, we would note the number of children interviewed in the previously discussed research project who used their drawings as an important additional means of extending and triggering their responses to the questions being asked. One child's decision to change his preferred role in the future from that of an ambulance driver to a racing car driver, for instance, evolved out of his drawing (male, five years and six months). Another child's narrative evolved in direct response to what he was drawing. By discussing the details of the drawing at hand, he triggered his memory and refined his understanding of the concepts with which he was engaging:

> Now just do the seats. Oh yeah, I know how to do seats, they're easy. See. I just have brown, brown. Better, oh yeah, this is going to be inside the ship. Inside will be upstairs and outside's downstairs. OK, one seat. There oh, this seat didn't have something over the top of it. The seats on the Tasmanian cat we were on had something over it.
>
> (male, five years and three months)

More is involved here than merely that children are frequently more comfortable working with drawings than they are with talking to adults without any visual stimulus. The children's visual orientation provides a further indication of their relative freedom from the narrowness and restrictiveness of many adult frameworks of thinking (Masini nd: 81–2). One of the limitations which they do not share is the adult tendency to place greater weight on the presumed logic of words above images.

The challenging and, at times, fundamental insights encountered in the visual arts eloquently attest to the failings of this perspective. Children share with visual artists an ability to forge new links and to gain new perspectives on the world by exploring their ideas in visual terms. The child cited above, for example, was able to create a new fantasy role model on the basis of the forms suggested by his drawing. Another child noted the resemblance between the leaves which she was drawing and the appearance of musical notes. She also commented, after completing her drawing of the world in the future, that the top of the drawing resembled a noughts and crosses game (female, five years and ten months, Figure 8). Her freedom of thought enabled her, in this instance, to make connections between images and concepts which adults frequently miss. Visual imagery should thus form a fundamental component of any curriculum which is designed to place value on fresh ways of perceiving and interpreting the future.

Visual imagery has an important futures-orientation in that it provides children with a significant means of reinterpreting existing concepts in new ways. One instance of this was the decision taken by the children I worked with to create their own Sistine Ceiling after I had described Michelangelo and the Sistine Chapel to them. The Ceiling took the form of life-sized outlines of the children's bodies which were coloured and placed in sequence on the ceiling of the kindergarten. This highly unusual and inventive conjunction of forms, which appeared to float on the ceiling, suggested to the children the forms of parachutists falling to earth. The meaning of the ceiling was changed, accordingly, in order to reflect this new concept.

What is striking about this anecdote is the degree to which it illustrates, once again, the children's signal ability to reinterpret existing concepts in new and innovative ways which, nonetheless, maintained a personal relevance to the children. The common adult response to Renaissance art is one of awestruck reverence and a sense of historical and cultural discontinuity (an attitude which facilitates the construction of the Old Master myth of genius). This was entirely absent from the children's understandings. The gulf of time and reputation was effortlessly dissolved as the children decided to try this creative idea for themselves. The new exhibition space of a kindergarten ceiling then suggested to them an entirely new concept which they followed with equal confidence and positivity. The example provides a powerful illustration of the way in which the use of images encourages the principles of flexibility and creativity which are so commonly stressed in futures studies.

A facility with visual images will also assist children to comprehend symbolic forms. Symbols are fundamentally important tools of educational communication since they form the basis of our understanding of language and mathematics (Dyson 1990: 50–7). Young children continuously draw upon symbolic images and gestures in order to communicate ideas and embellish story-lines in socio-dramatic play. There are many possibilities for the use of symbols in a programme. Symbols can be used to identify songs, for example, or to identify whether it is raining or sunny on weather charts. Dramatic play has also been highlighted as assisting children to learn symbols. This was further reinforced as a result of my working with a group of children who were fascinated by the topic of arms and armour. The children eventually decided to devise their own coats of arms after we had explored the idea of heraldry as a means of identifying families. These coats of arms rapidly evolved into a new language for the group which resulted over time in the children frequently including representations of their coats of arms beside their names or even using them as an identifying substitute for a signature. In this instance, as in the example of the Sistine Ceiling exercise, the children were able to use visual imagery as a means of expressing their sense of involvement in and ownership of the educational programme, feelings which are crucial to the previously stated objective of strengthening the children's self-concepts.

A number of ancillary skills are to be developed through the use of visual images in the educational programme. Some early childhood educators have discussed the value of museums, for example, as a means of promoting observational skills and aesthetic appreciation (Payne 1989: 12–14; Cole and Schaefer 1990: 33–8; Wolf 1990: 39–43; Piscitelli 1991: 197). They have noted that experiences of this kind can assist in the development of the children's sense of shapes and stylistic development and their ability to match, pair and sequence, and to define, describe and analyse line, colour, form and sensory properties. It would also assist them to interpret objects, articulate thoughts, appreciate other points of view and to extend their powers of logical and creative thinking (Cole and Schaefer 1990: 34–8; Wolf 1990: 39–43; Payne 1993: 101–16). Barbara Piscitelli notes the importance of museums for young children in their ability 'to capture the imagination and provoke thought ... and present young children with new ideas and opportunities for communication and expression' (Piscitelli 1991: 199). The importance of connecting with objects on a perceptual, intellectual, symbolic, sensory and emotional level has also been stressed in aesthetic educational studies as a means of enabling children to exert a sense of attachment and control over the wider socio-cultural environment.

- *For children to explore the concepts of continuity and change*

Recent studies have underlined that by four years of age children are generally able to reflect on and report the manner in which their earlier beliefs
have changed (Gopnick and Slaughter 1991: 98–110). Conversely, pre-school
children also have the ability to consider some of the ways in which they
might change in the future. We might recall here the example of the five-
year-old girl whose comment on the future was that it would be a time when
she went to school and learned 'lots of things that you can't understand
when you're a little kid' and that when children grow up they become 'more
truthful and things' (female, five years and six months).

In common with their adult counterparts, young children need to be able
to feel in control of change. If encouraged to view change positively young
children will not consider it separate and threatening to their lives. Change
forms part of the continuity of the children's world and can therefore be
welcomed as offering new possibilities for the future. Change, for pre-school
children, has the potential to be treated as an extension of their sense of
connectedness to the outside world.

Explorations of change occur constantly in the early childhood curriculum.
Scientific experiments, such as freezing and melting, explorations of life
cycles, growth and the seasons, or cooking experiences all underline the
concepts of change and adaptation. The cycles of the seasons also contain
within them the themes of continuity and change. Planting trees and
vegetable gardens and observing what remains the same and what continues
to change within the environment across the seasons can help to sustain this
focus throughout the year.

The relevance of these concepts can be emphasised once early childhood
professionals understand their significance in the wider picture of the
futures-orientation of the child's development. The tadpole does not simply
grow into a frog: the tadpole changes into a frog and yet remains the same
organism. Through this, children are able to see in a focused and easily
comprehensible example the dynamism of the principles of change and
continuity unfolding before their eyes. This kind of activity provides children with the opportunity to engage actively with the concept of change and
then to apply that knowledge to their wider experience of life. The key factor
in these considerations is that the child be given the opportunity to feel in
control of change and, by extension, of the future.

History provides a further means of addressing the concept of change at
the pre-school level. Hurst has argued that history can be addressed in a
concrete manner with young children as it is linked with their own sense of
identity (Hurst 1991: 3). The ego-centric nature of four-year-olds enables
them to perceive their own development in relation to the growth and development of the family and the community. The exploration of history can
enable children to develop a sense of the passing of time and of the past and

the present. It also encourages the development of logical and imaginative thinking. Henson has argued along similar lines that stories are invaluable tools for promoting a sense of time and chronology. The sequences that occur within stories and the signalling of events through repeated phrases such as 'once upon a time' help children to develop a sense of the passage of time and continuity (Henson 1991: 21–4). The children's own histories could be explored in this respect in the form of a series of photographs of their lives from birth. These might give them a vivid sense of the passage of time and of growth and change in a manner which is, once again, personally relevant to them. Photographs of the children in the centre and on excursions can also help to act as a trigger for the memory of the group. Lella Gandini describes how the Reggio Emilia educators incorporate photographs into their programmes:

> Most of the time these displays include, next to the children's work, photographs that tell about the process, plus a description of the various steps and evolution of the activity or project. These descriptions are meaningfully completed with the transcription of the children's own remarks and conversation that went along with their particular experience (which is often tape-recorded). Therefore, the displays ... provide documentation about specific activities, the educational approach, and the steps of its process.
>
> (Gandini 1998: 175)

The early childhood professional should, at the same time, be continually mindful of the need to frame each exploration of a futures-oriented issue in a manner which is developmentally appropriate to the children attending the programme. This is particularly true of such abstract and challenging concepts as the interrelationship of change and continuity and the interconnectedness of the past, the present and the future.

A good example of how the abstract concept of the interconnectedness of time can be translated into a developmentally appropriate experience for four-year-olds is the calendar in use at the College of Education Lab School of the University of Hawaii. Each day at this centre the children take turns to enter onto paper, individually, in pairs or in small groups, what they consider to be the significant aspects of the day. The paper on which they write and draw forms part of an extended roll which is unrolled at regular intervals throughout the year in order for the children to walk through and discuss what they have identified as the past, the present and the future of one year. The initiative, once again, allows the children to explore time in a manner which emphasises its direct connection with them. Time is not abstract, since the events and concepts placed on the time-scale are those which the children themselves have identified and depicted on their communally owned time-roll. Time is given a sense of stability and definition, since the recorded events remain on the paper as historical records. Yet time equally remains a fluid and ongoing continuum extending infinitely into the bound-lessness implied in the act of unravelling.

An initiative of this kind could give rise to the exploration of a number of futures related concepts (Van Scoy and Fairchild 1993: 24). Change and continuity could be discussed in similar terms in the light of seasonal change and experiments such as the observed growth cycles of animals or plants. The exploration of futures could be drawn out in terms of possible or preferable outcomes of experiments or other significant events occurring in the learning environment. In so doing, the direct relevance of the future in the present could be emphasised in concrete terms to the children.

Cathie Holden's work with seven-year-olds offers early childhood profes-sionals another potential learning experience incorporating a futures orientation. Holden uses time-lines with children as a means of emphasising the significance of human choice in the construction of possible and prefer-able futures (Holden 1989: 5–9). The children are asked to record significant historical events onto a piece of paper and to provide two tangents suggesting the probable and preferable outcomes of these events. This simple exercise underlines the importance of human thought and action in the construction of futures. It could be easily translated in terms of direct rele-vance to four- and five-year-olds, either in relation to possible outcomes of experiments or stories, or more directly in terms of the children's own lives.

A greater sense of the significance and relevance of these approaches can be achieved if we draw on research findings on the four-year-old's memory of the past. Research undertaken by William Friedman has demonstrated that, while four-year-olds have an understanding of the relative distance of different past events, they find it difficult to locate these events on conven-tional time-scales stretching longer than a day. Friedman has argued from this the need for young children to develop a representational time pattern which can be used to structure the past (Friedman 1991: 153). The use of activities that focus on children ordering patterns and sequences of events which are of direct relevance to them is thus of some importance since it assists them to gain a sense of a chronological past.

Such conceptual underpinnings can then be used as a means of projecting events into the future. Puzzles which require children to place in sequence events such as getting dressed, the growth of a seed into a tree and a tadpole into a frog can provide a further means of developing these skills. Discussing the sequence of events in story-lines can also help to develop these concepts and can offer children the scope to elaborate upon and change story-lines.

Activities of this kind, should, at the same time, be combined with explo-rations of the interconnectedness of time, such as in the previously discussed example of the time-roll used in the educational programme of the College of Education Lab School of the University of Hawaii. This would assist early childhood professionals to maintain an appropriate balance between extending the children's understanding of the conventional 'adult' perception of time, while also respecting their own more fluid, natural approach to time.

The curriculum foci discussed thus far constitute a series of skills and outlooks to help foster in children a sense of agency and ongoing engagement with their developing abilities to negotiate successfully the challenges and possibilities set up by the prospect of the future. At the same time, children will benefit equally from an emphasis on some of the broader and deeper values and attitudes which might strengthen and underpin the development of these skills. Accordingly, the following chapter will turn to consider the place of appropriate futures-oriented values in driving the early childhood curriculum.

Chapter 7

Applying futures values to the early childhood curriculum

Recent political and economic reforms in many countries have opened up new perspectives for education for international understanding and peace, human rights and democracy. In certain cases even, because of the need to root the reforms in people's values and attitudes, education is considered to be at the 'epicentre of the entire reform process'.

(Unesco 1995: 79)

Curriculum foci for futures-oriented values

- *For children to develop an awareness and tolerance of other individuals and cultures*
- *For children to identify common needs and shared interests with different cultures and individuals*
- *For children to develop a respect for diversity*
- *For children to develop an understanding of rights*

A central theme to emerge out of this discussion thus far, is the importance of the early childhood professional developing skills to deal with diversity. It is of equal importance that we develop the ability to instil in the children a responsiveness to these same concerns. Article 29 of the Convention on the Rights of the Child highlights an emphasis on individual and cultural diversity as fundamental to instilling in children a sense of mutually tolerant citizenship in a free society. An emphasis on respecting others will also involve early childhood professionals in celebrating the differing knowledge and skills brought by children into educational settings. These include language, cultural heritages and life experiences, as well as differing skills, abilities, interests and outlooks. To recognise these features by making them visible in the curriculum will bring about the additional benefit of assisting children and their families to feel that they have something important to contribute to the educational setting. The importance of ensuring that children from all ethnic, religious and linguistic groups have opportunities to enjoy their culture, to practise or profess their religion and to use their language with others is also highlighted in Article 30 of the Convention of the Rights of the Child.

A number of futures researchers have stressed the importance of global education as a means of implementing futures issues in the curriculum. Johnson has identified global education as an important means of encouraging children to analyse world-views (Johnson 1993: 3–13). For Fisher and Hicks, its importance lies in the manner in which it assists children to align their personal futures with their global futures (Fisher and Hicks 1985: Preface). This aim is to be achieved by first stimulating children's interest in the world and then by assisting them to understand their relationship to it. Futures issues can also be addressed in the context of exploring alternative global futures and the processes which need to occur in order to realise these alternatives (Fisher and Hicks 1985: 132–6; Pike and Selby 1988: 63–9, 279–81). Skills and attitudes which have been identified as stemming from a global studies perspective include interdependence, participation, cultural enrichment, respect, empathy, critical skills, self-awareness, cooperation, equality and a sense of justice. Studying different cultures, their reciprocal influences, their perspectives and ways of life will also be an important means of achieving a respect for diversity. The connections between global education and environmental studies and gender equity have also been stressed (Hicks and Steiner 1989: 2–10).

All these perspectives build on the fundamental issues of rights and equality and tolerance: 'If we are to achieve a sustainable future, then cooperation and social integration must be prioritised over aggression and individualism' (Siraj-Blatchford and Patel 1995: 122). The development of tolerance should constitute an important component of an educational curriculum with these foci. Reardon defines tolerance as 'according others the right to have their persons and identities respected' (Reardon 1997a: 14). Respect will form the basis from which cross-cultural understandings and reconciliation can be learned. Batelan speaks in a related sense of the need for intercultural understanding which is based on the values of 'international understanding, recognition and respect for cultural differences, issues of human rights and citizenship, the provision of equal opportunities and strategies for equal access to the learning processes in order to achieve equality of outcomes' (Dubbeldam et al. 1994: 123).

A number of early childhood educators have commented on the importance of global education. Eder and her colleagues have argued that young children possess 'global, context [and] independent concepts of themselves … [and] have the ability to maintain a stable, continuous record of who they are' (Eder et al. 1987: 1050) Caldwell has also posited that the early childhood curriculum is an appropriate context for the exploration of cultural, ethnic and religious diversity (Caldwell 1985b: 389). Phillips has argued, more broadly, that educators need to use global education as a means of examining the implications of institutional racism, oppression and the concept of culture. This examination, he suggests, needs to occur before early childhood and primary educators can foster cultural understanding and sensitivity in children (Phillips 1988: 42–7).

Susan Fountain has addressed the issue of how these concepts could be applied systematically in early childhood curricula. Fountain has asserted that global education can significantly assist the development of children's self-esteem and skills of communication and cooperation (Fountain 1990: 4). These concepts have an application across the curriculum and can form the foundations of learning at subsequent levels of education. One of the most important insights of Fountain's study is her suggestion that the objectives of global education can be achieved by defining those elements of the children's life experiences which relate to broader world issues. As an example of this, Fountain notes that the instance of young children calling each other names which are sometimes gender- or race-related can provide the educator with an opportunity to explore the concept of prejudice with the children.

A number of other parallels could also be drawn in this context. The occurrence of children excluding others from play for arbitrary reasons could form the occasion for an exploration of the concept of discrimination. The common occurrence of children arguing over materials could provide an opportunity for discussing the issue of resource distribution. Fights among children could be used as a forum for the discussion of the issue of peace and conflict. The discovery among children that more can be accomplished by sharing and working together could be used as a means of demonstrating the principle of interdependence. The negotiation between children in order to arrive at an agreed solution to a dispute could be used as a means of introducing the concept of cooperation and the importance of being conscious of other perspectives. Protest among children that rules are unfair could lead to a discussion of human rights. The use of consumable materials in a sometimes environmentally thoughtless manner can generate discussion on environmental awareness (Fountain 1990: 3–4).

Fountain's argument is of considerable use to the educator for its suggestion that the macro dimension of global issues can be explored through the micro dimension of the children's own experiences. This emphasis is similar to the previous discussion of the ways in which environmental issues and the concepts of change and continuity can be framed within specific learning experiences. Setting up the learning environment with posters and books which celebrate cultural diversity, together with stamps, coins and cooking experiences, can also facilitate the growth of these understandings.

- *For children to appreciate other points of view, to cooperate and to resolve conflicts peaceably*

• *For children to develop a sensitivity towards other children's needs and feelings*

Peace education is closely related to the objectives of global education. Like global education, it seeks to foster in children an understanding of human rights in relation to the children's needs and rights, the environment, conflict and cooperation, and multiculturalism (Sundgren 1983: 17).

The futures-orientation of peace education has been recognised by David Hicks in his definition of peace education as a framework for addressing 'problems of conflict and violence on scales ranging from the global and national to the local and personal'. The goal of the exploration of such concepts should, he suggests, be to consider ways of creating more just and sustainable futures (Hicks 1988: 5). Sundgren and Shoji have stressed the importance of exploring these issues at the early childhood and early primary levels of education since it is at this stage that lifelong values and attitudes towards 'races' are formed (Sundgren 1983: 9; Shoji 1992: 4). This is supported by Katz who believes that racial awareness begins from as early as two years of age (Katz, cited in Derman-Sparks and the ABC Task Force 1989: 2).

Numerous educators and researchers have stressed the need to manage conflict constructively and to deal with issues peaceably (Kreidler 1984; Conflict Resolution Resources for Schools and Youth 1985; Schmidt and Friedman 1985; Fry-Miller and Myers-Walls 1988). The conceptual underpinnings of peace can be developed at the early childhood level of education through experiences of security, independence, cooperation, understanding of others and sensitivity towards racial diversity (Shoji 1992: 4–9). Kreidler identifies cooperation, communication, tolerance, positive emotional expression and conflict resolution as particularly important skills and qualities for children to develop. Reardon cites a Unesco document that argues the need for children to develop the 'capacities for tolerance, living with diversity, dealing constructively with conflict, exercising responsibility' (Reardon 1997a: 26). The importance of the early childhood professional in modelling behaviour to the children takes on an added significance in this regard, in the light of a recent study conducted by Oboodiat. Oboodiat found that, while five- and six-year-olds have the capability to understand and value the concept of racial diversity, they have not yet fully developed the means to resolve conflicts non-violently (Oboodait 1993: 35).

Young children are, at the same time, generally well equipped to develop a respect for other cultures and points of view. As Flavell and others have noted, the ability in young children to appreciate and assess social mores and conventions is relatively well developed by the ages of four and five (Flavell *et al.* 1992: 960, 973–5). They are thus ready to begin to consider the means by which they might participate in the creation of a democratic and just educational setting which, Greenberg argues, should be one of the fundamental goals of education. In order to achieve this, early childhood professionals will need to foster in children the development of a number of skills and attitudes. These include an understanding of other perspectives and other people's rights and feelings, communication skills and an appreciation of consequences (Greenberg 1992: 14–17). She argues the importance of maintaining the children's sense of self-respect since it encourages the development of a concomitant sense of responsibility to consider the rights of others. A sense of the importance of responsibility encourages children to consider the role of ethics in their lives. It also strengthens a sense of pluralism as responsible individuals are able to accept the validity of differing points of view without coming into conflict with others.

- *For children to develop an understanding of others regardless of gender, race, class or disability*

   Children are aware very young that color, language, gender, and physical ability differences are connected with privilege and power. They learn by observing the differences and similarities among people and by absorbing the spoken and unspoken messages about those differences. Racism, sexism and handicappism have a profound influence on their developing sense of self.

                    (Derman-Sparks and the ABC Task Force 1989: ix)

A futures-oriented approach to early childhood education would also advocate equal opportunity for children regardless of their gender, race, class or disability. Vale and Roughead have emphasised the importance of an inclusive curriculum, particularly as it applies to interactions between children and the subjects offered at school (Vale and Roughead 1987: 58–61). Gender equity is of particular importance given that the sex role stereotypes introduced to children in the first years will influence how they view female and male roles throughout their lives. Numerous commentators in the field of early childhood education have accordingly stressed the differences between girls and boys in these years. Some have sought to demonstrate the degree to which early sex role stereotyping is evident in aspects of the children's interactions with others and how these issues can be explored in the early childhood curriculum (MacNaughton 1993a: 4–5). How children experience their bodies and their social environments will also influence their attitudes towards disabilities (Derman-Sparks and the ABC Task Force 1989: 2). It is of critical importance that early childhood professionals seek to foster in young children anti-bias attitudes toward disability and that they correspondingly seek to empower young children with disabilities to feel themselves to be valued members of the early childhood community so as to create an inclusive community (Derman-Sparks and the ABC Task Force 1989: 39).

An awareness of the significance of equity will help the early childhood professional to ensure that children are receiving the same experiences, that they can develop similar skills and positive attitudes towards each other regardless of gender, race, class or disability. It also helps to underline the importance of respecting diversity and difference in others which is commonly stressed as one of the principal tenets of futures education. In addition to ensuring that they present knowledge from different perspectives, it is important that early childhood professionals structure their learning environments to ensure that all children will have equal opportunities to participate in educational experiences. This will involve them in the process of reflecting on their own values and practice within educational settings in order to ensure that no racial or gender prejudice is present in the learning environment. Early childhood practitioners will also need to recognise and develop strategies to support the 'unique identities, understandings and styles of learning', that children and their families bring with them into the programme (Siraj-Blatchford 1995: 53). They will need to ensure that all children are treated fairly by each other and that behaviour management/ disciplinary policies place children's rights as central to the agenda, are non-discriminatory and reflect human dignity and that these ideals are reflected in policy statements (Siraj-Blatchford 1995: 49). How the curriculum is managed in relation to the elements of time, space and materials will also have a critical effect on the effective translation of these ideals. This emphasis will also help to develop a respect for human rights and fundamental freedoms, principles enshrined in the Convention on the Rights of the Child, the Convention on Discrimination in Education as well as the Charter of the United Nations.

- *For children to respect and identify with the natural environment*

We have previously noted the link which is frequently established between futures education and environmental awareness. Both futures studies and environmental studies, for example, stress the importance of individuals assessing the role of change and sustainability (Kinnear *et al.* 1989: 40–1, 50–1). The children's interviews cited in Chapter 2 provided further testimony to the fact that four- and five-year-old children often consider environmental issues. A study of three- and four-year-olds' understandings of biological growth found that both age groups demonstrated an understanding that animals and plants healed through regrowth and that this quality of growth distinguished animate from inanimate objects (Backscheider *et al.* 1993: 1242–57). Lavanchy's research into four- to six-year-olds has also underlined the extent to which an active engagement with the environment constitutes an important means by which children construct knowledge and perceive relationships within environments (Lavanchy 1993: 40).

The potential applications of environmental studies extend to all aspects of the curriculum. Environmental study can heighten a sense of visual acuity in children and provide them with an additional means of experiencing shape, point, line, rhythm, texture, form, pattern, colour and tone (Joicey 1986). It can also be used to explore the concepts of interrelationships, diversity, continuity and change, cooperation and inquiry-based learning (Gough 1988b: 10–17). Annette Greenall Gough speaks of the sensory delight to be gained from the environment and the active learning opportunities it offers. By developing an appreciation of ecology, she argues, children become committed to the environment. Environmental education can become an important medium with which to empower children to 'see their present circumstances more clearly and to act for a better future for themselves, their society and their earth' (Greenall Gough 1990: 60–5). Siraj-Blatchford and Patel highlight the importance of fostering in children 'a sense of wonder' about nature to achieve these aims (Siraj-Blatchford and Patel 1995: 122). Animals also constitute an important subject through which children might be encouraged to feel connected to their wider environment. The task of caring for animals and observing their growth offers children numerous opportunities both to feel in control of the environment and also to respect its needs. Establishing gardens can perform a similar function.

Environmental awareness also empowers children by offering them the means to put their ideas into action. An example is Janet Manning's project which sought to explore with four- and five-year-old children the principles adopted in Ray Lorenzo's work. Manning's project involved her and the children in an examination of the local playgrounds in order to identify what aspects they enjoyed and what aspects they wished to change. Designs were taken to the mayor who invited them to choose the equipment they preferred for the local park (Manning 1990: 34–8). The children involved in this project were given a sense that their feelings were recognised by adults who were committed to putting their ideas into action. Manning notes that a wide range of learnings occurred through this process. These included an increased sense of spatial awareness, an examination of gender roles in relation to the playground equipment, social awareness and responsibility, and decision-making skills. Manning notes that the children undertaking the project:

> learnt to discuss ideas and to really listen to each other and appreciate another person's point of view. They began to think and question more, rather than simply accepting and taking every situation at face value. I encouraged them to come up with solutions and they discovered that they were really very good at this.
>
> (Manning 1990: 37)

In this example the nurturing of understanding and respect for the natural environment represents a tangible way in which children can come to feel connected to natural processes. It can further build on the children's experience and sense of interdependence, diversity, continuity and change, and in so doing develop an awareness of the delicate balance and interrelationships that can exist in communities. These experiences will assist in reinforcing in children a sense of control of their world. An early childhood curriculum that allows children to plan for the environment and see an outcome will also enable children to experience further that their ideas can be put into action and have additional benefits for others.

Conclusion

Implementing futures-focused curricula in the field of early childhood education enables early childhood professionals to consider how much real decision-making they place in the hands of the children when setting up learning environments and planning curricula. How responsive are professionals to children's requests to change the environment in some way in order to render it more personally relevant and responsive to their differing needs? What values and attitudes are being modelled and shaped within the programme? To what extent does the curriculum reflect the diversity of concerns and life experiences of the children and families attending the programme? How much value and time do professionals place on exploring possibilities with children? How many choices do early childhood professionals offer the children during the course of a session? How flexible are professionals in adapting the structure, space and content of the programme to meet the changing needs, interests and abilities of the children? Futures concerns provide an important means of opening the curriculum out to the children in order to make it more accessible to them without, at the same time, sacrificing its educational integrity.

Futures studies also encourages early childhood professionals to consider their own feelings towards the future and attitudes towards their roles in shaping the future. Early childhood professionals need to ask themselves how committed they are to coming to terms with these issues and acting upon them through their work with children. They also need to give consideration to their own feelings towards the future before they can begin to work with the children in this regard. It is appropriate, therefore, that we shift our attention to the adult educators themselves as a means of assessing some of the ways in which they can reflect on the issues articulated in studies of this kind.

Chapter 8

Early childhood professionals as agents of change

An analysis of futures studies in early childhood education needs to focus closely and systematically on the attitudes and interests of young children. But other factors need also to be taken into account when considering the implementation of a futures-oriented early childhood oriented curriculum. Consideration should also be given to the implications of the initiative for the practitioners themselves. It is they, after all, who will be responsible for translating futures concerns in ways which are sensitive to the wider contexts in which children grow. It is worth while, therefore, to examine some of the current challenges and considerations facing the application of a futures-oriented early childhood curriculum.

It is important, in the first instance, to recognise the gap that currently exists in both the fields of early childhood education and futures studies. We have already noted that the findings of futures studies research remain, with very few exceptions, unintegrated with early childhood curriculum research. It should also be recognised that futures studies is not, at present, being taught at the level of teacher training. Early childhood professionals accordingly remain largely unaware of the relevance of futures studies to curriculum formulation. The lack of research and writing in the area has tended to exacerbate the problem, resulting in the production of very little accessible information on the topic. A programme of research, teacher training, in-service training and publications will need to be developed in order to offer support to those early childhood educators who wish to address issues of this kind. An emphasis on continued educational training is integral to the ongoing professional development of early childhood professionals, particularly when they become more experienced practitioners of their professions (Katz 1995: 209; Rodd 1998: 17). Programmes of this kind might also benefit from drawing on pre-service and in-service training as a means of assisting staff to develop new competencies which might help them to understand the implications involved in the application of innovative curricula (De La Cruz and Maclean 1990: 3–14).

Another important factor limiting the development of futures studies in early childhood education is that it may be seen to challenge the traditional procedures developed by early childhood professionals. The principles of futures education are, as we have seen, commensurate with many of the principles already inherent in early childhood education. Futures studies, nonetheless, offers a new conceptual framework with which to reassess children's knowledge, growth and learning. It requires the assimilation of a new educational approach which, while cohesive, is also interdisciplinary in nature. It also requires that practitioners reconsider their educational philosophy and the methods by which they formulate curricula. Some degree of self-scrutiny will be required in order to sustain the process of reworking and refining the existing frameworks of the curriculum. In essence, the implementation of a futures-oriented curriculum will require early childhood professionals to develop within themselves the skills and attitudes which they wish to instil in children (Wallis 1979: 121). As Masini has noted, futures educators must first clarify their own understanding of the world and their position within the many alternatives for the future before they can fruitfully address these issues with young children (Masini 1986a: 7). Holland has noted that such a process will involve early childhood practitioners in a process of re-educating and re-training the collective skills and capacities of the discipline (Holland 1993: 60).

Watts has stressed, in a related sense, the need for professionals to understand the implications of the broader social issues relating to the future. She observes that the early childhood educator's knowledge of child development and growth should include what she terms a 'contemporary validity', noting that:

> The early childhood professional must be aware not only of trends in society but also of the variations in response to their social and personal context and to the fact of change itself by individual adults and children. Out-of-date stereotypes generated by texts and teachings which were based on earlier life styles, situations, adjustments and child-rearing practices must not be replaced by new stereotypes; the professional must see beyond the generalisation to the individual.
>
> (Watts 1987: 9)

This process will carry with it inevitable implications for professional development. Early childhood professionals seeking to develop programmes of this kind will need to develop further their ability to respond professionally to changes in social and educational contexts, to implement innovations successfully, to broaden their understanding of the social significance of education and to deepen their understanding of contemporary society (Board of Teacher Education in Queensland Report, 'Project 21: Teachers to the Twenty-First Century', cited in Watts 1987: 11; Clyde, 1984: 4–8).

Halliwell and MacLean have also pointed to the need for early childhood educators to take into account the broader social contexts in which they teach (Halliwell 1992b: 131; MacLean 1992: 44). An orientation of this kind, they argue, would encourage early childhood professionals to consider seriously what they wish young children to learn. Such self-reflection could serve to extend their understanding of the potential for young children to develop skills of long-term developmental significance.

The implementation of a futures-oriented early childhood curriculum would also involve early childhood professionals in the process of reappraising the manner in which they interact with children in order to impart values, attitudes and knowledge. Such an emphasis would see early childhood practitioners engaged in an ongoing process of reflective teaching. Professionals engaged in reflective teaching will evaluate their teaching methods in order to think 'carefully about what they are doing and saying and not saying in the daily interactions with children and question what children have or have not learnt from these interactions' (MacNaughton and Williams 1998: xi). A central part of this process involves listening to the children on matters that concern them in the early childhood programme and adapting the learning environment in response to them so that 'the children are not shaped by experience, but are the ones who give shape to it' (Malaguzzi 1998: 86). The benefits of critical reflection in early childhood programmes have been noted in the wider research literature and are wide-ranging (MacNaughton and Williams 1998: xi–xii). Collectively they point to a greater responsiveness to individual children and a greater equality of outcomes for children regardless of class, gender, ethnic and ability groups.

In addition to the practical outcomes for the community of children attending an early childhood programme, critical reflection also assists early childhood professionals to share their knowledge of teaching and learning with others (Brown 1996: 8). An ability to reflect on and discuss curriculum priorities will result in early childhood practitioners raising the profile of young children and the importance of systematically addressing in their educational frameworks issues relating to children's long-term growth and development.

Advocacy and the early childhood curriculum

We have explored the ways in which a futures-oriented curriculum might help to infuse the educational setting with a responsiveness to longer-term perspectives of child growth and learning, and might also help to place these issues in a broader context. In the current Australian climate, for example, where a national curriculum is being mooted at the level of early childhood education, educators will need to be able to address publicly and systematically how the curriculum can best suit the needs of young children. Futures studies offers the field a potentially highly appropriate framework within which to address these issues.

An awareness of the relevance of futures concerns will also assist professionals to understand the wider agendas at work in the early childhood service provision (Halliwell 1992b: 130). Insights of this kind will enable early childhood practitioners to advocate more effectively for the rights of young children. The concept of advocacy requires that early childhood professionals recognise and adopt that which is most beneficial for the children. In so doing, it places a special emphasis on the vulnerability of young children and the special relationship of trust that evolves with adults in order to ensure that their needs and rights are being heard and met: 'We can act as catalysts to help others understand children's needs as our collective responsibility and our shared future' (Goffin and Lombardi 1988: 5).

In order to achieve this aim, early childhood professionals will need to develop a public voice for children and demonstrate the importance of early childhood educational programmes for children's long-term development. An awareness of the wider political processes which inform the educational setting and children's lives, and a readiness to engage with these processes will better equip educators to remain true to the principles of advocacy: 'we need to begin by more fully understanding the cultural, economic, and political transformation of our society and its institutions if we are to reduce the disadvantages they create and maximise the opportunities they present' (Sharpe 1999: 5).

A major challenge facing the implementation of these initiatives is the lack of cohesion and unity that has existed within the field of early childhood education. In Australia, for example, the historical separation of education from care has led to a dichotomy within the discipline which has tended to detract from a recognition of the field's true professional status (Scutt 1992: 31–45). If the early childhood profession is to be taken seriously it needs to assess critically the arbitrary nature of such divisions and to develop strategies which might engender a greater sense of unity across the field. Futures frameworks provide appropriate rationales for such an endeavour by placing the children back on the main agenda and by directing the profession as a whole towards a consideration of its shared objectives and concerns. At the same time, futures frameworks also allow for a due emphasis to be given to the diversity which exists within the early childhood profession.

The implementation of futures concerns in the early childhood curriculum will be influenced, to a major degree, by the setting in which early childhood professionals work. The field of early childhood is characterised by a broad range of service models which cater for the differing needs of the clientele within the community. They vary from long-day programmes to sessional and occasional programmes in centres as well as the family-based option of family day care. These services all have different orientations and receive differing degrees of funding from different levels of government. The professional context in which early childhood professionals find themselves should thus also be taken into account when examining further the means by which futures concerns are to be adopted in early childhood education. Consideration needs to be given, for example, to the issues involved in applying these frameworks in group teaching environments.

The level of training will also affect the early childhood professional's ability to embrace new philosophical and methodological frameworks. This varies in early childhood services according to the kind of service under which one is employed. The educator's ability to appreciate the principles of futures studies and their relevance to early childhood education will be affected by his or her knowledge of child development, understanding of the principles underlying curriculum development and experience in formulating and implementing curricula. These experiences and understandings will also, in turn, influence early childhood professionals' perceptions of themselves as advocates for young children. Early childhood practitioners will also have different needs at different stages of their professional development. These considerations will be more likely to be taken up by early childhood professionals after they have conquered the initial practical challenges of the workplace (Katz 1995: 209; Rodd 1998: 22–3). The importance of a rigorous undergraduate training on these issues will help to ensure that they become more central to practitioners' considerations throughout their development.

Coming to terms with innovation and change

> The early childhood field in Australia is not renowned for its ability to initiate change [or to], develop new directions or futuristic perspectives. We have always tended to be reactive rather than proactive.
>
> (Lambert 1994: 1)

Experience would suggest that there is a wide range of factors influencing the manner in which early childhood professionals respond to curricula innovations. Most innovations require a change either in the practitioners' outlooks or in the strategies which they adopt in the learning environment. The value that professionals place on an innovation will have a direct bearing on its level of success (Brown and McIntyre 1978: 19; Johnson nd: 9). Olson stresses, in this regard, the ability of curriculum change to challenge educators' pre-existing beliefs and practices (Olson 1980: 1). Factors influencing the practitioner's commitment to an innovation include the extent to which the objectives of an innovation match the educator's beliefs, the perceived organisational obstacles to its implementation, the immediate relevance of an innovation to the educator's daily concerns and the extent to which the innovation satisfies the social and parental expectations placed on the children. The satisfaction or interest which the educator derives from the innovation will also play a role in determining the success of the innovation's implementation (Brown and McIntyre 1978: 19–20).

Crandall has stressed the importance of practitioners feeling in control of an educational innovation and its methods of implementation (Crandall 1983: 9). Educators will also need to be able to translate a pedagogical innovation into practical learning experiences (Brown and McIntyre 1978: 21). Gusky and Johnson have both underlined the importance of staff development programmes as a means of assisting educators in this task (Gusky 1986: 6; Johnson nd: 21). This issue requires further consideration since, as has previously been noted, there have been very few concrete examples outlined for the practical application of futures studies in the early childhood educational context.

A major factor influencing the success of the implementation of an innovation is the degree to which it requires a change in the roles and relationships between the individuals in the organisation (Fullan and Pomfret 1977: 337). Early childhood professionals' relative autonomy is an advantage in this regard. Early childhood educators who adopt futures concerns will not be required to alter radically their relationships with staff, clients and management. The process of change would thus be easier to implement because it would be contingent on the cooperation of fewer people and institutions than would be the case for primary and secondary school educators.

Personality has also been identified as an influence on the ability of educators to re-negotiate their professional knowledge (Sieber 1972: 362–8, cited in Olson 1980: 2). The implementation of a futures-oriented curriculum requires that early childhood professionals re-examine their own prejudices and biases concerning the future and their place within it. For many individuals this process can be fraught with tension as it requires them to grapple with their fears and uncertainties as well as with the concepts of change and adaptation.

Slaughter has devised a useful framework with which to address the nature of change and the reconceptualisations of meaning involved in the process of undergoing change. This model, which he terms the T-Cycle, identifies four key stages of change: the breakdown of meaning, reconceptualisation, negotiation and conflict, and the final stage of selective legitimation (Slaughter 1986: 39). Breakdowns in meaning occur when assumptions are questioned and challenged by the reconceptualisations or new meanings that evolve. Negotiation or conflict results from the individuals processing and critically engaging with the issues brought about by change, and selective legitimation occurs as some proposals are accepted and new levels of perception and understanding are achieved. These stages are similar to those outlined by Johnson and Owen in a recognition of the existing teaching repertoire of moving through refinement, re-examination and renovation prior to reaching a stage of renewal where the educator re-evaluates the nature, extent and use of his or her repertoire and plans additions as necessary (Johnson 1989: 8).

Early childhood professionals and the research agenda

An important means of raising our awareness and understanding of issues concerning the implementation of a futures-focused early childhood curriculum is to involve the practitioners themselves in the process of reflecting and researching their own practice. They are, after all, dealing constantly with the practical realities of the processes which futures-oriented curricula seek to address. It thus becomes critical in an under-researched area such as the implementation of a futures-oriented early childhood curriculum, that the broader research agenda incorporates the perspectives of the professionals themselves. Such an emphasis will assist us to explore further the complexity of issues that practitioners may face in successfully integrating these concerns into their curricula.

In a small attempt to begin to address this issue, I interviewed four early childhood professionals employed in a work and community-based early learning centre across ten months of the calendar year. Staff were chosen on the basis of their commitment to incorporating futures concerns in their curriculum frameworks. A group of early childhood professionals were provided with an introductory session on futures studies and the early childhood curriculum, and provided with a booklet of readings. Following an interval of time in which they thought through these issues, individual members assessed whether they would be interested in becoming involved in the project. Four staff volunteered their services and were interviewed individually approximately every six weeks during which time they shared issues that they had documented in their journals over the period. Each of the staff interviewed were in their early to mid-twenties and had worked in early childhood settings for three to eight years.

Alice

Alice felt that a great deal of what she was seeking to achieve with the children had a futures-orientation, but she had not had the philosophical or methodological frameworks to understand how to translate this in practice. A key part of the process of formulating a futures-focused curriculum involved Alice in reflecting on her values concerning children and relating them to the key tenets underlying the philosophical frameworks of futures studies. Alice spoke of the importance of providing a choice of open-ended activities for children as this encouraged problem-solving and allowed for self-directed learning as well as strengthening their self-esteem by creating an affirming and meaningful learning environment for the children.

A further benefit of analysing the long-term benefits of the skills she was developing in the children was that it would offer her a framework for discussing with parents the importance of developing skills, values and attitudes in terms of the children's long-term development. Alice believed that early childhood professionals are under a great deal of pressure to conform to parents' expectations to teach an academic programme to the children. This created a tension for her in terms of how she could negotiate a curriculum with the families attending her programme.

> The hard part is keeping up with the parent's expectations. I want to be able to feel at peace with what I'm doing with the children. I want to be able to feel that it is right. A couple of times I haven't felt that, I feel that it's too oriented and too product-related. I want to be able to do what I think is right for the children and to justify that to the parents and to my staff and explain and feel confident that this is right for the children, right for the children not only for now but for the future.

In the past Alice had felt frustrated and hindered by trying to justify the need to plan for qualities such as flexibility and adapting to change to parents. Part of the difficulty she felt was that these were qualities that couldn't be displayed on walls and thus weren't visible to the parents. Long-term qualities are not readily perceived in the present. Futures studies, she believed, could provide a solid rationale and an important vehicle through which to explain the relevance of the qualities to the parents in terms of their children's long-term growth and development.

Convincing parents of the need for a less overtly structured and academically oriented programme would have the added benefit of releasing her from the pressure of constantly having to prepare the children academically for school.

> I find children need a lot of imaginative and creative play and I think that is really important. I feel that I need to interact with the children all the time and that I have to be teaching them content rather than working on skills that they need to learn in future. Sometimes I think I should really get the children to do something and they do it but I think I'm getting them to do that for the adults and I think what are they getting out of this? Sometimes I think we are stifling them a little bit and directing their learning.

Alice stressed the importance of role modelling in a futures-oriented programme:

> What children need for the future is caring and happiness and the building of a positive outlook towards the future. So I think that can be done by having a positive outlook yourself, like being a happy person and having a bit of joke and a sense of humour and being really aware

of prejudice and treating all children equally, make sure you treat all children equally, so they learn to treat all their peers equally.

Alice also cited the example of modelling a positive attitude in the garden as a means of building children's respect for the natural environment. A futures-oriented early childhood curriculum for Alice would focus on flexibility, the ability to adapt to change, the importance of a high self-esteem, creative and lateral thinking, active, creative and imaginative play. An early childhood learning environment would allow the children to feel safe to experiment and explore. It would also provide the children with a number of choices, the scope to direct their learning in a way that is meaningful to them and to feel secure, loved and valued in all their diversity. Children in this kind of educational setting would be awakened in a manner which would empower them to create change and to gain a real sense of self and of the world.

Heather

Heather was not initially convinced about the notion of a futures-based curriculum in early childhood. For Heather, this project shed some light on the potential of what she was doing with the children:

> At first I thought futures studies sounds so boring but when I really thought about it and broke it down and looked at it step by step I thought well really we are doing some of these things and looking at futures curriculum unconsciously rather than being aware of it. So then I went back and related it to some of the experiences we've been recently doing with the children.

As a result, Heather rewrote her philosophy statement in the light of her newfound recognition of the futures-based work that she had been undertaking with the children.

Heather's futures-oriented curriculum became more specific as she re-examined her work with the children in the light of the wider research literature. She moved from broad-based goals in her first interview (such as communication skills, environmental issues, encouraging children's awareness of growth and change) to more focused qualities such as open-mindedness, the need for inner direction and confidence and a positive self image, organisational skills, conflict resolution, cause and effect, and an understanding of the consequences of actions. As she discussed these skills she independently provided a futures-related rationale for all them. For example, when Heather spoke of consequences for action she stated: 'I would like that the children be able to understand that if they act in a particular way it is going to impact on other things [it] will have an impact on the future.'

Elizabeth

Elizabeth chose initially to focus on the key skills, qualities and outlooks which she would need to implement across the course of the year and how she might broadly conceptualise such a programme. She used the term 'life-centred,' to describe her futures-focused curriculum as a means of placing the children and their lifelong qualities central to the agenda. She accordingly incorporated this concept into her philosophy statement. Elizabeth also actively sought to integrate futures-oriented skills into her work with the children at the time of the interview as a way of testing the working model of a futures-based curriculum.

Elizabeth identified one of the advantages of this process as the stronger emphasis which it encouraged on her thinking critically about issues with the children. Her major response to the issues raised by the readings was to 'brainstorm' ideas with children and to use this approach as a means of conceiving a plurality of options, including inventive, creative and imaginative possibilities, and acknowledging the different viewpoints of the children in these sessions. An openness to learning and re-learning concepts and an attendant flexibility of thinking, she believed, were fundamental to this task both for the educator as well as for the children. A stronger priority of these processes saw Elizabeth reflect more fully on the notion of ownership of the curriculum and place a more explicit emphasis on negotiating the curriculum with the children and the families attending the programme: 'I've tried to empower them so that they can create their own environment.' She identified self-esteem as a critical foundation for a curriculum of this kind, which she described as the 'undercurrent determining thing of how they're going to think about themselves and their ideas'.

Elizabeth felt that the readings were very useful in terms of providing her with:

> a concrete understanding of futures curriculum. It is important and it is nice to have a vocabulary that some of these people are using and tuning that finely to an area like the futures curriculum, which also pervades the whole programme.

Elizabeth also found that she used different terminology with the children such as the past and the future as a means of giving children a reference point for the work they were undertaking together. She believed that the future in this manner could act as a symbolic language for the children. Elizabeth saw a futures-oriented curriculum as one which could provide great opportunities for the children and assist in the formulation of a meaningful educational environment for them.

Nicole

Nicole used the readings as a starting point for addressing a futures-oriented curriculum. She found that this initiated a process of self-reflection about 'how I was as a child to how I am now and the factors that influenced me on my way'. Through this process Nicole decided that a positive self-concept had been critical to her happiness and well-being and felt this was the cornerstone of a successful futures-oriented programme. She also felt the readings offered her a new perspective on the potential of what she could achieve with the children. A newfound sense of what was possible altered her educational programme for the children and saw her shift her orientation from simply planning for their current developmental needs to complementing this with a sense of their long-term development. It also facilitated a re-appraisal of her interactions with the children. She would use anecdotes of recent events within the programme and dissect them according to this newfound understanding of futures planning. Nicole felt this process had an important impact on her professional life, making her feel 'more positive in what I'm doing'. It resulted in a rewriting of her philosophy in which she stated the importance of the early childhood setting and curriculum in shaping children's futures.

Self-reflection had also highlighted for Nicole the importance of her acting as a positive role model for the children. She was particularly touched by the research literature on young people's attitudes to the future and felt it was important for professionals to be conscious of the values they instil in young children. She noted that if you want to give them a good head start, then you need to reconcile your own feelings towards the future otherwise your ambivalence or fears would be unconsciously picked up by the children. This reflection, Nicole believed, would ultimately result in a positive culture of socialisation occurring in early childhood programmes.

Nicole noted the skills children need for the future from the wider readings she had consulted and reflected on whether she was addressing them in her programme. The skills she felt were of particular importance in this regard included flexibility, learning how to assert change, problem-solving, creativity, imagination, skills of communication and decision-making, independence, cooperation, choice, conflict resolution, taking responsibility for actions, talking about emotions and showing appreciation of other children. Nicole found that as she identified these skills her current work with the children changed in its emphasis and was given a renewed sense of direction and purpose.

Key themes arising out of the research

Each of the professionals undertaking the project found the task of attempting to formulate a futures-oriented curriculum a worthwhile endeavour that resonated with their understanding of the purpose and potential of the early childhood curriculum. The process offered these practitioners a new perspective through which to consider what they were already implicitly attempting to address in the curriculum. A fuller examination of the research literature in this area provided them with the impetus to reflect more fully on what they were seeking to achieve with the children and their level of success in realising their aims. All four believed they should plan for young children's futures, but at the same time this was not an explicit thrust of their educational programme. Nor was a futures-oriented rationale being employed to justify educational experiences for the future. The research literature provided an important foundation in this regard and was used by all four professionals as a means of identifying futures-related skills, and as a means of considering how these skills might be extended so as to remain relevant to the children's futures. As a result, each member re-examined and sharpened their focus on what they were seeking to achieve with the children and the means by which they went about achieving it.

This process ended in all four professionals rewriting their philosophy statements in the light of these new perspectives. Changes in their philosophy statements reflected new images of children, new perspectives on the importance of early childhood educational frameworks in laying lifelong foundations and a stronger sense of professional responsibility in this regard. Other outcomes of the process included a renewed confidence in discussing the curriculum with the parents by providing a rationale for their curriculum foci, a stronger thrust on allowing children to co-design a curriculum and a different sense of how they could interact with children to reinforce futures-based perspectives. In all, these new insights and perspectives were having an impact on the early childhood community as they were working through these issues.

Conclusion

The perspectives raised in this chapter have served to highlight the potential benefits to be gained from implementing a futures-focused curriculum in early childhood education. It is a task which is rendered all the more pressing by the fact that the discipline of early childhood education has not yet systematically formulated the methodologies necessary for a sustained examination of its fundamental objective to lay important foundations for future growth and learning. The time for such an assessment is now long overdue. The children attending early childhood programmes are poised at a crucial stage of their development. Early childhood professionals need to reflect on their educational practice with children, their families and the wider community so that they can consider how best to refine their knowledge and skills in order to respond to the current and future needs, growth and development of young children.

This study recognises the challenges that remain for a full assessment of the concerns raised in these chapters. Further research needs to be undertaken into young people's attitudes towards the future. Additional consideration is required of how pre-school children perceive the future and how early childhood professionals can plan and implement programmes that address these understandings. The application of futures studies in a variety of educational contexts is also necessary before it will be possible to draw out fully the implications of implementing curricula with this focus. Further research is also required on how early childhood professionals and parents can work together on these issues so that they can be translated in a manner that is sensitive towards the different service provision and clientele for whom they cater.

Yet there can be no doubting the degree to which this undertaking can contribute significantly to the early childhood professional's fundamental task of establishing positive foundations for future growth and learning. It can provide practitioners with a methodology with which to explain, justify and add meaning to the importance of their work. It constitutes a new framework in which to address issues such as accountability, professionalism and advocacy. In short, it provides a new ethic within which to frame issues of direct significance to present and future generations of children.

Bibliography

Agarwal, A. and Tiwari, S. (1988) 'Future Orientation: A Mediator in Temporal Coding', *International Journal of Psychology*, 23: 151–63.

Agius, E. (ed.) (1994) *Why Future Generations Now?*, Kyoto: Institute for the Integrated Study of Future Generations.

Albery, N. and Mill, C. (eds) (1986) *Best Ideas: A Dictionary of Social Inventions*, London: Institute for Social Inventions.

Albery, N. and Yule, V. (eds) (1989) *Encyclopaedia of Social Inventions*, London: Institute for Social Inventions.

Allen, D.W. and Plante, J. (1980) 'Looking at the Future of Education', in L. Jennings and S. Cornish (eds) *Education and the Future*, Bethesda: The World Future Society.

Alley, J.D. (1985) 'Futures Research Data and General Education Reform', paper presented at the 25th Annual Forum of the Association for Institutional Research, Portland, Educational Resources Information Center, 1985.

Amara, R. (1981) 'The Futures Field: Searching for Definitions and Boundaries', *The Futurist*, 15: 25–9.

Anderson, B.E. (1992) 'Effects of Day Care on Cognitive and Socioemotional Competence of Thirteen-Year-Old Swedish Schoolchildren', *Child Development*, 63: 20–36.

Apple, M.W. (1983) 'Curriculum in the Year 2000: Tensions and Possibilities', *Phi Delta Kappan*, 5: 321–6.

Archard, D. (1993) *Children: Rights and Childhood*, London: Routledge.

Arthur, L., Beecher, B., Dockett, S., Farmer, S. and Death, E. (1996) *Programming and Planning in Early Childhood Settings*, Sydney: Harcourt Brace.

Ashby, G. (1988) 'Early Childhood Education: Past, Present, Future', *Links*, 2: 4–8.

Associazione L'Età Verde, *Come gli studenti vedono i problemi mondiali*, Rome: Edizioni L'Età Verde.

Ausburn, F.B. and Ausburn, L.J. (1993) 'Some Affirmative Views on Technology in Education', *Unicorn*, 6, 1: 25–34.

Australian Curriculum Studies Association (1993) 'Vision for Australian Schooling', *Curriculum Perspectives*, 13, 2: 43–8.

Australian Early Childhood Association (1991) 'The Australian Early Childhood Association Code of Ethics', *Australian Journal of Early Childhood*, 16, 1: 3–6.

Backscheider, A.G., Shatz, M. and Gelman, S.A. (1993) 'Preschoolers' Ability to

Distinguish Living Kinds as a Function of Regrowth', *Child Development*, 64: 1242–57.

Bäckström, K. (1992) 'Children's Rights and Early Childhood Education as Reflected in the Convention of the Rights of the Child', *International Journal of Early Childhood*, 24, 1: 22–6.

Baier, K. (ed.) (1969) *Values and the Future: The Impact of Technological Change on American Values*, New York: The Free Press.

Balson, M. (1981) 'Preparing Personnel to Work in the Early Childhood Field in the '80's', *Australian Journal of Early Childhood*, 6, 2: 24–8.

Barnes, R.E. (1978) 'An Educator Looks Back From 1996', *The Futurist*, 12, 2: 123–6.

Barthes, R. (1972) *Mythologies*, London: Vintage.

Beare, H. (1984) 'Education and the Post-Industrial State', *Unicorn*, 10, 2: 127–40.

—— (1990) *An Educator Speaks to his Grandchildren: Some Aspects of Schooling in the New World Context*, Canberra: Australian Council for Educational Research, Monograph Series 8.

Beare, H. and Slaughter, R.A. (1993) *Education for the Twenty-First Century*, London: Routledge.

Bell, W. (1971) 'A Paradigm for the Analysis of Time Perspectives and Images of the Future', in W. Bell and J.A. Mau (eds) *The Sociology of the Future*, New York: Russell Sage Foundation.

—— (1983) 'An Introduction to Futuristics: Assumptions, Theories, Methods, and Research Topics', *Social and Economic Studies*, 32, 2: 1–64.

Bell, W. and Mau, J.A. (1971) 'Images of the Future: Theory and Research Strategies', in W. Bell and J.A. Mau (eds) *The Sociology of the Future*, New York: Russell Sage Foundation.

Benjamin, S. (1989) 'An Ideascape for Education: What Futurists Recommend', *Educational Leadership*, 7, 1: 8–14.

Benne, K.D. (1990) *The Task of Post-Contemporary Education: Essays on Behalf of the Human Future*, New York: Teachers College Press.

Bennett, A. *et al.* (1992) 'A Developmental Examination of Adolescents' Fears', *Canadian Journal of School Psychology*, 8, 1: 69–79.

Berenson, B. (1981) *Aesthetics and History*, London: Constable.

Berk, L. (1997) *Child Development*, Boston: Allyn and Bacon.

Berman, L.M. (1984) 'Educating Children for Lifelong Learning and a Learning Society', *Childhood Education*, 61, 21: 363–9.

Berman, L.M. and Roderick, J.A. (1977) 'Future Curricular Priorities', *Educational Research Quarterly*, 1, 4: 79–87.

Berman, M. (1984) *The Reenchantment of the World*, New York: Bantam Books.

Bernard Van Leer Foundation (1989) *The Challenge: Early Childhood Care and Education, an Agenda for Action*, The Hague: Bernard Van Leer Foundation.

Bexson, A. (1991) 'Imaginative Play and History Teaching', *Early Years*, 12, 1: 20.

Bickel, D., Zigmond, N. and Strayhorn, J. (1991) 'Chronological Age at Entrance to First Grade: Effects on Elementary School Success', *Early Childhood Research Quarterly*, 6, 2: 105–17.

Birch, C. (1975) *Confronting the Future, Australia and the World: The Next Hundred Years*, Melbourne: Penguin Books.

Blunt, A. (1962) *Artistic Theory in Italy, 1450–1600*, Oxford: Oxford University Press.

Botkin, J.W., Elmandjra, M. and Malitza, M. (1979) *No Limits to Learning: Bridging the Human Gap, a Report to the Club of Rome*, Oxford: Pergamon Press.

Boucouvalas, M. (1983) 'Lifelong Learning and the Information Society', paper presented at the Education and the Information Age Conference, Falls Church, VA (Educational Resources Information Center, ED244144).

Boulding, K.E. (1969) 'The Interplay of Technology and Values: The Emerging Superculture', in K. Baier and N. Rescher (eds) *Values and the Future*, New York: Free Press.

Boulding, E. (1973) 'Futurology and the Imagining Capacity of the West', in F. Tugwell (ed.) *Search for Alternatives: Public Policy and the Future*, Cambridge: Winthrop.

—— (1989) 'The Dynamics of Imagining Futures', in R.A. Slaughter (ed.) *Studying the Future: An Introductory Reader*, Melbourne: Commission for the Future and the Australian Bicentennial Authority.

Bowman, J., Dede, C. and Kierstead, F. (1980) 'Educational Futures: A Reconstructionist Approach', L. Jennings and S. Cornish (eds) *Education and the Future*, Bethesda: The World Future Society.

Boyer, W. (1997/8) 'Playfulness Enhancement through Classroom Intervention for the 21st Century', *Childhood Education*, 74, 2: 90–6.

Brant, R. (1983) 'On Education and the Future: A Conversation with Harold Shane', *Educational Leadership*, 41, 1: 11–13.

Bredekamp, S. (1991) 'Redeveloping Early Childhood Education: A Response to Kessler', *Early Childhood Research Quarterly*, 60, 2: 199–209.

Bronfenbrenner, U. (1979) *The Ecology of Human Development: Experiments by Nature and Design*, Cambridge, MA: Harvard University Press.

Brown, R. (1996) 'Teacher Reflections on Educational Theory and Practice', in *Weaving Webs: Collaborative Teaching and Learning in the Early Years Curriculum*, Conference Proceedings, Melbourne: Department of Early Childhood Studies, Faculty of Education, University of Melbourne.

Brown, S. and McIntyre, D. (1978) 'Factors Influencing Teachers' Responses to Curricular Innovations', *British Educational Research Journal*, 4, 1: 19–23.

Burdin, J.L. and Nutter, W. (1984) 'Inventing the Future: Options and Strategies for Educators', paper presented at the Annual Meeting of the American Association of Colleges for Teacher Education, San Antonio (Educational Resources Information Center, ED240119).

Cahen, S. and Cohen, N. (1989) 'Age versus Schooling Effects on Intelligence Development', *Child Development*, 60: 1239–49.

Cairns, R.B., Cairns, B.D. and Neckerman, J. (1989) 'Early School Dropout: Configurations and Determinants', *Child Development*, 60: 1437–52.

Caldwell, B.M. (1985a) 'Issues for the Future: How do we Teach for Tomorrow?', guest editorial, in A.M. Gordon and K. Browne (eds) *Beginnings and Beyond: Foundations in Early Childhood Education*, New Jersey: Delmar Publications.

—— (1985b) 'Issues and Trends in Early Childhood Education', in A.M. Gordon and K. Browne (eds) *Beginnings and Beyond: Foundations in Early Childhood Education*, New Jersey: Delmar Publications.

—— (1988) 'Early Childhood Education in the 21st Century', *Child Care Information Exchange*, 64, December: 13–15.

Cannella, G.S. (1997) *Deconstructing Early Childhood Education: Social Justice and Revolution*, New York: Peter Lang.

Capra, F. (1983) *The Turning Point: Science, Society and the Rising Culture*, London: Flamingo, Fontana Paperbacks.

Carter, D.S.G. (1986) 'Examining the Implementation of a Curriculum Innovation: A Centre–Periphery Example', *Curriculum Perspectives*, 6, 1: 1–6.

Centre Georges Pompidou (1987) *Atelier des enfants*, Paris: Centre Georges Pompidou, Atelier des enfants.

Chandler, M., Fritz, A.S. and Hala, S. (1989) 'Small-Scale Deceit: Deception as a Marker of Two-, Three-, and Four-Year-Olds' Early Theories of Mind', *Child Development*, 60: 1263–77.

Chasle, R. (1987) *The World by the Year 2000*, Paris: Unesco, Bureau of Studies and Programming Major Programme 1, Reflection on World Problems and Future-Oriented Studies, Studies and Documents.

Cirlot, J.E. (1961) *A Dictionary of Symbols*, London: Routledge and Kegan Paul.

Clark, K. (1961) *Looking at Pictures*, London: John Murray.

—— (1969) *Civilisation: A Personal View*, London: British Broadcasting Corporation.

—— (1981) *Moments of Vision*, London: John Murray.

Clark, T. (1988) 'Believing is Seeing – Not the Reverse', *The Quest*, Autumn: 49–56.

Clarke, I.F. (1979) *The Pattern of Expectation 1644–2001*, London: Book Club Associates.

Claydon, L.F. (1984) 'Curriculum and Technology: Against Disinheriting Youth', *Curriculum Perspectives*, 4, 1: 1–7.

Cleverley, J. and Phillips, D. (1987) *Visions of Childhood: Influential Models from Locke to Spock*, Sydney: Allen and Unwin.

Clyde, M. (1984) 'Pre-Schools for the Next Century', *Links*, 4: 4–8.

—— (1989a) 'Early Childhood for the Future: From "Hothouse" to "Greenhouse"', *Australian Association of Early Childhood Educators' Newsletter*, 30: 5–16.

—— (1989b) 'A Lifelong Curriculum for Children of Preschool Age', paper presented to the Eastern Metropolitan Region Children's Services Office, Adelaide, 23–7 October.

Coates, J.F. and Jarret, J. (1992a) *What Futurists Believe*, Washington, DC: Lomond Publications Inc./World Future Society.

—— (1992b) 'Exploring the Future: A 200-Year Record of Expanding Competence', *Annals of the American Academy*, AAPS, 522, July: 12–24.

Coggin, P.A. (1979) *Education for the Future: The Case for Radical Change*, Oxford: Pergamon Press.

Cohen, D. (1991) 'Speaking across the Gender Gap', *New Scientist*, August: 30–2.

Cole, S. (1995) 'Contending Voices: Futures, Culture and Development', *Futures*, 27, 4: 473–81.

Cole, E. and Schaefer, C. (1990) 'Can Young Children Be Art Critics?', *Young Children*, January: 33–8.

Coles, M. (1991) 'Creating a Community of Inquiry: Philosophy for Five-Year-Olds', *Early Years*, 12, 1: 33–6.

Comber, J.P. (1984) 'Home–School Relationships as they Affect the Academic Success of Children', *Education and Urban Society*, 16, 3: 323–37.

Combs, A.W. (1981) 'What the Future Demands of Education', *Phi Delta Kappan*, January: 369–72.

Commission for the Future (1987) *Future Options*, Melbourne: Commission for the Future.

—— (1988) *Perspectives on Australia's Future, An Annotated Bibliography and Accompanying Monograph on 'Review of Australian Studies to the Year 2000'*, prepared for Unesco, Regional Office, Bangkok, Melbourne: Commission for the Future.

Condry, S. and Marquart, J. (eds) (1983) *As the Twig is Bent … Lasting Effects of Preschool Programs*, Hillsdale, NJ: Lawrence Erlbaum Associates and the Consortium for Longitudinal Studies.

Conflict Resolution Resources for Schools and Youth (1985) *Conflict Managers' Training Manual for Grades 3–6*, San Francisco: The Community Board.

Coombs, P.H. (1982) 'Critical World Educational Issues of the Next Two Decades', *International Review of Education*, 28.

Cornish, E. (1977) *The Study of the Future*, Washington, DC: World Future Society.

Crandall, D.P. (1983) 'The Teacher's Role in School Improvement', *Educational Leadership*, 41, 3: 6–9.

Crawford, A. (1992) 'Painting a New Picture', *21.C*, 8, Summer: 78–81.

Crunden, D. *et al.* (1989) 'Investigating the Future: A Resource Book for the Secondary Classroom', manuscript prepared for publication by the Commission for the Future and the Australian Bicentennial Authority, Melbourne.

Cryon, J.R., Sheehan, R., Wiechel, J. and Bandy-Hedden, I.G. (1992) 'Success Outcomes of Full-Day Kindergarten: More Positive Behaviour and Increased Achievement in the Years After', *Early Childhood Research Quarterly*, 7, 2: 187–203.

Cumming, J. (1994) 'Educating Young Adolescents: Targets and Strategies for the 1990s', *Curriculum Perspectives*, 14, 3: 41–4.

Dahle, K. (1991a) 'Participatory Futures Studies Concepts and Realities', paper presented at the 12th World Conference of the World Futures Studies Federation, Advancing Democracy and Participation: Challenges for the Future, Barcelona, 17–21 September.

—— (1991b) *On Alternative Ways of Studying the Future: International Institutions, an Annotated Bibliography and a Norwegian Case*, Oslo: The Alternative Future Project.

—— (1998) 'Towards Governance for Future Generations. How do we Change Course?', *Futures*, 30, 4: 277–92.

Dau, E. (1991) 'Let's Pretend: Socio-Dramatic Play in Early Childhood', in S. Wright (ed.) *The Arts in Early Childhood*, New York: Prentice Hall.

Davie, R. (1993) 'Listen to the Child: A Time for Change', *The Psychologist*, June: 252–7.

De Jong, P.F. (1993) 'The Relationship between Students' Behaviour at Home and Attention and Achievement in Elementary School', *British Journal of Educational Psychology*, 63, 2: 201–13.

De Jouvenal, B. (1973) 'A Word to Futurists', in Rome World Special Conference on

Futures Research, *Human Futures, Needs, Societies, Technologies*, Guildford: *Futures*, IPC Science and Technology Press Ltd.

De La Cruz, L. and Maclean, R. (1990) 'Implications of Megatrends in Curriculum Reform at the School Level in Asian-Pacific Countries for the New Competencies Required of Teachers', *Pacific-Asian Education*, 2, 1: 3–14.

De Loache, J.S. (1991) 'Symbolic Functioning in Very Young Children: Understanding of Pictures and Models', *Child Development*, 62, 4: 736–52.

Delors, J. *et al.* (1996) *Learning: The Treasure Within*, Report to UNESCO of the International Commission on Education for the Twenty-First Century, Paris: Unesco.

Derman-Sparks, L. and the ABC Task Force (1989) *Anti-Bias Curriculum. Tools for Empowering Young Children*, Washington, DC: NAEYC.

De Vries, A. (1974) *Dictionary of Symbols and Imagery*, Amsterdam: North Holland Publishing Company.

Didsbury, H.M. (ed.) (1984) *Creating a Global Agenda: Assessments, Solutions and Action Plans*, Washington, DC: World Future Society.

Digby, P. (1983) 'Children and the Threat of Nuclear War: Survey of Sydney School Children', commissioned by the Medical Association for the Prevention of War (Australian Branch).

Dockett, S. and Perry, B. (1996) 'Young Children's Construction of Knowledge', *Australian Journal of Early Childhood*, 21, 4: 6–11.

Doll, W.E. (1989) 'Foundations for a Post-Modern Curriculum', *Journal of Curriculum Studies*, 21, 3: 243–53.

Drake, M. and Drake, W. (1916) *Saints and their Emblems*, London: T. Werner Laurie Ltd.

Dresden, J. and Myers, B.K. (1989) 'Early Childhood Professionals: Toward Self-Definition', *Young Children*, 44, 2: 62–6.

Dubbeldam, L.F.B. (1994) *International Yearbook of Education, volume XLIV – 1994 Development, Culture and Education*, prepared for the International Bureau of Education. Paris: Unesco.

Dyson, A.H. (1990) 'Symbol Makers, Symbol Weavers: How Children Link Play, Pictures, and Print', *Young Children*, January: 50–7.

Ebbeck, M. (1983) 'The Pre-School Curriculum: Its Relevance for Children and Their Future Needs', *Australian Journal of Early Childhood*, 8, 3: 9–12.

—— (1991) 'National Reform in Education in Australia: Some Implications for Early Childhood Education', *Early Childhood Education and Care*, 77: 37–45.

Eckersley, R. (1988a) *Australian Attitudes to Science and Technology and the Future: A Report to the Commission for the Future*, Canberra: Australian Government Publishing for Commission for the Future.

—— (1988b) 'Casualties of Change: A Postscript', *In Future*, 11, Dec.: 16–18.

—— (1988c) *Casualties of Change – The Predicament of Youth in Australia: A Report on the Social and Psychological Problems Faced by Young People in Australia*, Canberra: Australian Government Printing Service for Australia.

—— (1990–1) 'Violence Rising', *21.C*, Summer: 64–6.

—— (1992) *Apocalypse? No! Youth and the Challenge to Change: Bringing Youth, Science and Society Together in the New Millennium*, Melbourne: Commission for the Future.

—— (1997) 'Portraits of Youth: Understanding Young People's Relationship with the Future', *Futures*, 29, 3: 243–9.

—— (1999) 'Dreams and Expectations: Young People's Expected and Preferred Futures and their Significance for Education', *Futures*, 31, 1: 73–90.

Eder, R.A. (1990) 'Uncovering Children's Psychological Selves: Individual and Developmental Differences', *Child Development*, 61: 849–63.

Eder, R.A., Gerlach, S. and Perlmutter, M. (1987) 'In Search of Children's Selves: Development of the Specific and General Components of the Self-Concept', *Child Development*, 58: 1044–50.

Edwards, P. (1983) 'Social Demands and Future Education: A Critique of Core Curriculum', Unicorn, 9, 1: 21–7.

Edwards, C.P. and Gandini, L. (1989) 'Teachers' Expectations about the Timing of Developmental Skills: A Cross-Cultural Study', *Young Children*, 44, 4: 15–19.

Edwards, C.P., Gandini, L. and Forman, G. (eds) (1998) *The Hundred Languages of Children: The Reggio Emilia Approach – Advanced Reflections*, Norwood: Ablex Publishing.

Elkind, D. (1981) 'All Grown Up and No Place to Go', *Childhood Education*, 58, 2: 69–72.

Erdley, C.A. and Dweck, C.S. (1993) 'Children's Implicit Personality Theories as Predictors of Their Social Judgements', *Child Development*, 64: 863–78.

Erickson, S.W. (1980) 'Education and the Creation of the Future', in L. Jennings and S. Cornish (eds) *Education and the Future*, Bethesda: The World Future Society.

Evans, O.W. (1985) 'A Backward Look at Future Directions in Education', *Curriculum Perspectives*, 5, 1: 25–31.

Feely, J. and Freeman, G. (eds) (1989) *Greenhouse Activity Materials, Primary*, Melbourne: Greenhouse Action Australia.

Fein, G.G. (1878) 'Technologies for the Young', *Early Childhood Research Quarterly*, 2, 3: 227–43.

Feshback, N.D. and Feshback, F. (1987) 'Affective Processes and Academic Achievement', *Child Development*, 58: 1335–47.

Fidock, A. (1985) 'Peace Education – Or Education for Peace?', *Curriculum Perspectives*, 5, 2: 64–7.

Field, T. (1991) 'Quality Infant Day-Care and Grade School Behaviour and Performance', *Child Development*, 62: 863–70.

Fingersten, P. (1970) *The Eclipse of Symbolism*, Columbia: University of South Carolina Press.

—— (1971) 'Symbolism and Reality', *Journal of Psycholinguistic Research*, 1, 1: 99–112.

Fisher, S. and Hicks, D. (eds) (1985) *World Studies 8–13: A Teacher's Handbook*, Edinburgh: Oliver and Boyd.

Flavell, J.H., Mumme, D.L., Green, F.L. and Flavell, E.R. (1992) 'Young Children's Understanding of Different Types of Beliefs', *Child Development*, 63, 4: 960–77.

Fleer, M. (1992) 'From Piaget to Vygotsky: Moving Into a New Era of Early Childhood Education', in B. Lambert (ed.) *Changing Faces: The Early Childhood Profession in Australia*, Watson: Australian Early Childhood Association.

Fleet, A. and Clyde, M. (1993) *What's in a Day? Working in Early Childhood*, Wentworth Falls: Social Science Press.

Fölster, K. (1999) 'The Place of Children in Fast-Changing Societies: Great Possibilities and Fatal Dangers?', *International Journal of Early Childhood*, 31, 1: 1–10.

Forbes, R.H. (1984) 'Thinking Skills: What Are They? Can They Be Taught? Why and How?', *NASSP Bulletin*, 68: 68–75.

Ford, S. (1980) *Redress the Education System*, Washington, DC: US Department of Education, National Institute of Education (Educational Resources Information Center, ED184996).

Fordman, P. (ed.) (1992) *Education for All: An Expanded Vision*, Roundtable Themes 11, World Conference on Education for All at Jomtein, Thailand, Paris: Unesco.

Foss, C. (1990) *Diary of a Spaceperson*, Limpsfield: Dragon's World.

Fountain, S. (1990) *Learning Together: Global Education 4–7*, Leckhampton: Stanley Thornes Ltd. and the World Wide Fund for Nature, Centre for Global Education.

Frank, L.K. (1966) 'The World as a Communication Network', in G. Kepes (ed.) *Sign, Image, Symbol*, London: Studio Vista.

Franklin, B. (1995) *The Handbook of Children's Rights: Comparative Policy and Practice*, London: Routledge.

Frede, E. and Barnett, S. (1992) 'Developmentally Appropriate Public School Preschool: A Study of Implementation of the High/Scope Curriculum and its Effects on Disadvantaged Children's Skills at First Grade', *Early Childhood Research Quarterly*, 7, 4: 483–99.

Freeman, J. (1992) *Quality Basic Education: The Development of Competence*, prepared for the International Bureau of Education. Paris: Unesco.

Frey, K.S. and Ruble, D.N. (1987) 'What Children Say about Classroom Performance: Sex and Grade Differences in Perceived Competence', *Child Development*, 58: 1066–78.

Friedman, W.J. (1991) 'The Development of Children's Memory for the Time of Past Events', *Child Development*, 62: 139–55.

Frost, R. (1986) 'Children in a Changing Society: Frontiers of Challenge', *Childhood Education*, 62, 4: 242–9.

Fry-Miller, K.M. and Myers-Walls, J.A. (1988) *Young Peacemakers Project Book*, Illinois: Brethren Press.

Frydenberg, E. (ed.) (1999a) *Learning to Cope: Developing as a Person in Complex Societies*, Oxford: Oxford University Press.

—— (1999b) 'Health, Well-Being and Coping? What's that to do with Education?', *Australian Journal of Guidance and Counselling*, 9, 1: 1–17.

Frydenberg, E. and Lewis, L. (1996) 'Social Issues: What Concerns Young People and How They Cope', *Peace and Conflict: Journal of Peace Psychology*, 2, 3: 271–81.

Fullan, M. and Pomfret, A. (1977) 'Research on Curriculum and Instruction Implementation', *Review of Educational Research*, 47, 2: 335–97.

Fuller, A., McGraw, K. and Goodyear, M. (1999) 'Bungy Jumping through Life: What Young People Say Promotes Well-Being and Resilience', *Australian Journal of Guidance and Counselling*, 9, 1: 159–68.

Funder, K. (ed.) (1996) *Citizen Child: Australian Law and Children's Rights*, Melbourne: Australian Institute of Family Studies.

Gandini, L. (1984) 'Not Just Anywhere: Making Child Care Centers into "Particular" Places', *Beginnings*, Summer: 17–20.

—— (1998) 'Educational and Caring Spaces', in C.P. Edwards, L. Gandini and G. Forman (eds) *The Hundred Languages of Children: The Reggio Emilia Approach – Advanced Reflections*, Norwood: Ablex Publishing.

Gandini, L. and Edwards, C.P. (1988) 'Early Childhood Integration of the Visual Arts', *Gifted International*, 5, 2: 14–18.

Garrett, M.J. (1993) '"A Way Through the Maze": What Futurists Do and How They Do It', *Futures*, April: 254–74.

Gawith, G. (1986) 'Information Skills for an Information Age?', *Unicorn*, 12, 2: 87–93.

Gay, G. (1981) 'Instructional Imperatives for the '80s', in L.V. Edinger, P.L. Houts amd D.V. Meyer (eds) *Education in the '80s: Curricula Challenges*, Washington, DC: National Education Association.

Germov, J. (1994) 'What to Do with the Working Class? Towards a Cultural Critique of the Curriculum', *Curriculum Perspectives*, 14, 1: 1–10.

Gibboney, R.A. (1989) 'Just Words: Talking Past Reform to Educational Renewal', *Journal of Curriculum and Supervision*, 4, 3: 230–45.

Gidley, J.M. (1998) 'Prospective Youth Visions through Imaginative Education', *Futures*, 30, 5: 395–408.

Gieldon, S. (1966) 'Symbolic Expression in Prehistory and in the First Civilisations', in G. Kepes (ed.) *Sign, Image, Symbol*, London: Studio Vista.

Gifford, R. (1984) 'Age, Era, and Life Perspective: Emotional Connotations of the 1920s through the 1980s to Individuals in their Twenties through their Eighties', *International Journal of Aging and Human Development*, 20, 1: 33–40.

Gjesme, T. (1983) 'On the Concept of Future Time Orientation: Considerations of Some Functions' and Measurements' Implications', *International Journal of Psychology*, 18: 443–61.

Glaser, R.G. (1975) 'The School of the Future: Adaptive Environments for Learning', in L. Rubin (ed.) *The Future of Education: Perspectives on Tomorrow's Schooling*, Boston: Allyn and Bacon.

Glines, D. (1978) 'What Competencies will be Needed in the Future?', *Thrust for Educational Leadership*, 7, 4: 24–5, 28.

—— (1991) 'Imagineering: Key to Educational Futures', Futurics, 15, 3–4, papers presented at the 1991 World Future Society Conference, Creating the Twenty-First Century: Individual Responsibility, Minneapolis.

Glover, A. (1999) 'The Role of Play in Learning and Development', in E. Dau (ed.) *Child's Play: Revisiting Play in Early Childhood Settings*, Sydney: Maclennan and Petty.

Godet, M., Bourse, F., Chapuy, P. and Menant, I. (1991) *Futures Studies: A Tool-Box for Problem Solving*, Paris: Futuribles GERPA.

Goffin, S.G. and Lombardi, J. (1988) *Speaking Out: Early Childhood Advocacy*, Washington, DC: NAEYC.

Gombrich, E.H. (1972) *Symbolic Images: Studies in the Art of the Renaissance*, London: Phaidon.

—— (1982) *The Image and the Eye: Further Studies in the Psychology of Pictorial Representation*, London: Phaidon.

Goodlad, J.I. (1973) 'A Concept of School in 2000 AD', in R.W. Hostrop (ed.) *Foundations of Futurology in Education*, Homewood: Etc. Publications.

Gopnik, A. and Slaughter, V. (1991) 'Young Children's Understanding of Changes in their Mental States', *Child Development*, 62: 98–110.

Gordon, T.H. (1992) 'The Methods of Futures Research', *Annals of the American Academy of Political and Social Science*, 522, July: 25–35.

Gough, N. (1981) 'Futures Study in Teacher Education', *South Pacific Journal of Teacher Education*, 9, 2: 48–57.

—— (1986) 'Futures in Curriculum', *Curriculum Perspectives*, 6, 2: 53–4.

—— (1987a) 'Alternative Futures in Environmental Education', *Environmental Education: Past, Present and Future*, Proceedings of the Third National Environmental Education Seminar and Workshops, Canberra: Australian Government Publishing Service, Department of Arts, Heritage and Environment.

—— (1987b) 'Forecasting Curriculum Futures: Acts of Anticipation in Curriculum Inquiry', paper presented at the Annual General Meeting of the American Educational Research Association, Washington, DC, 20–4 April.

—— (1988a) 'Children's Images of the Future: Their Meaning and Their Implications for School Curriculum', *Curriculum Concerns*, 5, 2: 6–10.

—— (1988b) 'Learning with Environments … An Ecological Paradigm for Education', *Green Teacher*, March: 10–17.

—— (1988c) 'Tacit, Token and Taken for Granted: The Concept of Futures in Australian Curriculum Work', *Unicorn*, 15, 1: 27–35.

—— (1989) 'Seven Principles for Exploring Futures in the Curriculum', in R.A. Slaughter (ed.) *Studying the Future: An Introductory Reader*, Melbourne: The Commission for the Future and the Australian Bicentennial Authority.

—— (1990a) 'Renewing our Links with Nature: Some Arts of Becoming Ecopolitical in Curriculum Work', *Curriculum Perspectives*, 10, 2: 66–9.

—— (1990b) 'Tacit, Token and Taken for Granted', *Futures*, April: 298–310.

—— (1994) 'Futures Education: For Whose Future?', *Primary Education*, 25, 5: 11–13.

Gould, S.J. (1987) *Time's Arrow, Time's Cycle: Myth and Metaphor in the Discovery of Geological Time*, Harmondsworth: Penguin.

Grant, J. (1998) 'A New Educational Paradigm for the New Millennium. Consciousness-Based Education', *Futures*, 30, 7: 717–24.

Graubard, A. (1972) *Free the Children: Radical Reform and the Free School Movement*, New York: Random House.

Green, H.B. (1975) 'Temporal Stages in the Development of Self', in J.T. Fraser and N. Lawrence (eds) *The Study of Time II*, Berlin: Springer-Verlag.

Green, T. (ed.) (1971) *Educational Planning in Perspective Forecasting and Policy Making*, Guildford: *Futures*, IPC Science and Technology Press Ltd.

Greenall Gough, A. (1990) 'Red and Green: Two Case Studies in Learning through Ecopolitical Action', *Curriculum Perspectives*, 10, 2: 60–5.

Greenberg, P. (1992) 'Ideas that Work with Young Children: How to Institute Some Simple Democratic Practices Pertaining to Respect, Rights, Roots, and Responsibilities in any Classroom (Without Losing Your Leadership Position)', *Young Children*, July: 10–17.

Greene, A.L. (1986) 'Future-Time Perspective in Adolescence: The Present of Things Future Revisited', *Journal of Youth and Adolescence*, 15, 2: 99–113.

Greene, M. (1986) 'In Search of a Critical Pedagogy', *Harvard Educational Review*, 56, 4: 427–41.

Greenwood, A. (1993) *Children's Rights: The United Nations Convention on the Rights of the Child*, AECA Resource Book, Series No. 4. Watson: AECA.

Greig, S., Pike, G. and Selby, D. (1987) *Earthrights: Education as if the Planet Really Mattered*, London: Kogan Page Ltd. and the World Wildlife Fund.

Griffin, P.E. (1985) 'Educational Futures: An Issue to be Considered Now', *Curriculum and Research Bulletin*, 20, 2: 10–29.

—— (1986a) 'Futures Research and Educational Planning', *Curriculum Perspectives*, 6, 2: 54–59.

—— (1986b) *Predicted Futures and Curriculum Change*, Melbourne: Victorian Ministry of Education.

Griffith, P.P. (1974) 'Teaching the Twenty-First Century in a Twentieth-Century High School', in A. Toffler (ed.) *Learning for Tomorrow: The Role of the Future in Education*, New York: Random House.

Grumet, M.R. (1981) 'Restitution and Reconstruction of Educational Experience: An Autobiographical Method For Curriculum Theory', in M. Lawn and L. Barton (eds) *Rethinking Curriculum Studies*, London: Croom Helm.

Gullo, D.F. and Burton, C.B. (1993) 'The Effects of Social Class, Class Size and Prekindergarten Experience on Early School Adjustment', *Early Childhood Development and Care*, 88: 43–51.

Gusky, T.R. (1986) 'Staff Development and the Process of Teacher Change', *Educational Researcher*, 15, 5: 5–12.

Haggis, S.M. (ed.) (1991) *Education for All: Purpose and Content*, Roundtable Themes 1, World Conference on Education for All, at Jomtein, Thailand, Paris: Unesco.

Hall, J. (1974) *Dictionary of Subjects and Symbols in Art*, London: John Murray.

—— (1983) *A History of Ideas and Images in Italian Art*, London: John Murray.

Halliwell, G. (1981) 'The Concept of Teaching in Early Childhood Education – Some Reflections', *Australian Association of Early Childhood Educators' Bulletin*, 15: 2–8.

—— (1989) 'Curriculum Implementation, Change and the Teacher of Young Children', paper presented at the Institute of Educational Research and Australian Early Childhood Association Conference, Learning and Early Childhood: How Important are the Early Years?, Sydney, June.

—— (1990) 'Infusing Critical Pedagogy into Early Childhood Teacher Education? A Response to Battersby', *Unicorn*, 16, 1: 47–51.

—— (1992a) 'Curriculum in Australian Care and Education Programs for Children Under Eight Years of Age', *Curriculum Perspectives*, 12, 3: 41–2.

—— (1992b) 'Practical Curriculum Theory: Describing, Informing and Improving Early Childhood Education', in B. Lambert (ed.) *Changing Faces: The Early Childhood Profession in Australia*, Watson: Australian Early Childhood Association.

Hamm, B. (1992) 'UNESCO's Associated Universities Project (UAUP)', *Futures*, June: 515–20.

Handley, H. and Samelson, A. (eds) (1988) *Child: Quotations About the Delight, Wonder, and Mystery of Being a Child*, New York: Penguin Books.

Harford, S. (1992) 'Graduating to the Year 2000: The Future of Education', *21.C*, 8, Summer: 82–4, 94.

Harman, W. (1988) *Global Mind Change: The Promise of the Last Years of the Twentieth Century*, Indianapolis: Knowledge Systems Incorporated.

Harper, L.V. and Huie, K.S. (1987) 'Relations among Preschool Children's Adult and Peer Contacts and Later Academic Achievement', *Child Development*, 58: 1051–65.

Hart, R. (1997) *Children's Participation: The Theory and Practice of Involving Young Citizens in Community Development and Environmental Care*, New York: Earthscans Publications.

Hatch, J.A. (1990) 'Young Children as Informants in Classroom Studies', *Early Childhood Research Quarterly*, 5, 2: 251–64.

Havighurst, R.J. (1974) 'The Future of Education: Image and Reality', in T.W. Hipple (ed.) *The Future of Education: 1975–2000*, Pacific Palisades: Goodyear Publishing Company Inc.

Hawking, S. (1988) *A Brief History of Time*, London: Bantam Books.

Hayes, D.S. (1992) 'Young Children and Television: The Retention of Emotional Reactions', *Child Development*, 63, 6: 1422–36.

Henderson, H. (1978) *Creating Alternative Futures: The End of Economics*, New York: Berkley Publishing.

—— (1986) 'The Three Guides of Transition: A Guide to Riding the Tiger of Change', *Futures Research Quarterly*, 2, 1: 19–37.

—— (1993) 'Social Innovation and Citizen Movements', *Futures*, April: 322–38.

Henry, M. (1996) *Young Children, Parents and Professionals: Enhancing the Links in Early Childhood*, London: Routledge.

Henson, S. (1991) 'Historical Stories and Historical Understanding', *Early Years*, 12, 1: 21–4.

Hicks, D. (ed.) (1988) *Education for Peace: Issues, Principles, and Practice in the Classroom*, London: Routledge.

—— (1991a) *Exploring Alternative Futures: A Teacher's Interim Guide*, London: Global Futures Project, Institute of Education, University of London.

—— (1991b) 'Preparing for the Millennium: Reflections on the Need for Futures Education', *Futures*, July–August: 623–36.

—— (1991c) 'Starting Points', in J. Smart (ed.) *My World: Exploring the Future*, Godalming: Scholastic Publications Ltd. on behalf of the World Wide Fund for Nature.

—— (1994) *Preparing for the Future: Notes and Queries for Concerned Educators*, London: World Wide Fund for Nature in association with Adamantine Press.

—— (1996a) 'A Lesson for the Future. Young People's Hopes and Fears for Tomorrow', *Futures*, 28, 1: 1–13.

—— (1996b) 'Retrieving the Dream: How Students Envision their Preferable Futures', *Futures*, 28, 8: 741–9.

—— (1997) 'From Foreclosure to Foresight', *Futures*, 29, 1: 98–9.

Hicks, D. and Holden, C. (1995) *Visions of the Future: Why we Need to Teach for Tomorrow*, London: Trentham Books.

Hicks, D. and Steiner, M. (eds) (1989) *World Studies 8–13 – Making Global Connections: A World Studies Workbook*, Edinburgh: Oliver and Boyd.

Hildebrand, V. (1991a) 'Families: A Global Perspective', *Early Childhood Development and Care*, 67: 53–60.

—— (1991b) 'Young Children's Care and Education: Creative Teaching and Management', *Early Childhood Development and Care*, 71: 63–72.

Hill, S. (1988) *The Tragedy of Technology*, London: Pluto Press.

—— (1989) 'Changing the Technological Trajectory – Addressing the Trailing Edge of Australia's Historical Culture', paper presented at the conference of the Centre for Applied Research on the Future, Futures for Australia and the Pacific, University of Melbourne.

Hills, T.W. (1987) 'Children in the Fast Lane: Implications for Early Childhood Policy and Practice', *Early Childhood Research Quarterly*, 2, 3: 265–73.

Hirsch, W.Z. (1969) 'Education and the Future', in R. Jungk and J. Jarratt (eds) *Mankind 2000*, Oslo and London: Universitetsforlaget and Allen and Unwin.

Holbrook, A. (1992) 'Teachers with Vision and Visions of Teaching: The Role of Futures Studies and Research in Post-Graduate Teacher Education', *Futures Research Quarterly*, 8, 4: 27–48.

Holden, C. (1989) 'Teaching about the Future with Younger Children', in R.A. Slaughter (ed.) *Studying the Future: An Introductory Reader*, Melbourne: The Commission for the Future and the Australian Bicentennial Authority.

Holland, S. (1993) 'Schooling for the Twenty-First Century', *Curriculum Perspectives*, 13, 3: 57–60.

Huber, B.J. (1971) 'Studies of the Future: A Selected and Annotated Bibliography', in W. Bell and J.A. Mau (eds) *The Sociology of the Future: Theory, Cases, and Annotated Bibliography*, New York: Russell Sage Foundation.

Hughes, F.P. (1995) *Children, Play and Development*, Boston: Allyn and Bacon.

Hughes, P. and MacNaughton, G. (1999) *Communication in Early Childhood Services: A Practical Guide*, Melbourne: RMIT Publishing.

Hunt, J. (1985) 'Education for Peace: A Curriculum for Global Action', *Curriculum Perspectives*, 5, 2: 68–71.

Hunt, J.B. (1983) 'Action for Excellence: Excerpts from the Task Force Report', *Educational Leadership*, 41, 1: 14–18.

Hurst, V. (1991) 'Teaching History to Young Children', *Early Education*, Spring: 3–4.

Hutchinson, F.P. (1996) *Educating beyond Violent Futures*, London: Routledge.

Hyson, M.C., Hirsch-Pasck, K. and Rescorla, L. (1990) 'The Classroom Practices Inventory: An Observation Instrument Based on NAEYC's Guidelines for Developmentally Appropriate Practices for 4–5-Year-Old Children', *Early Childhood Research Quarterly*, 5, 1: 475–94.

Inayatullah, S. (1990) 'Deconstructing and Reconstructing the Future: Predictive, Cultural and Critical Epistemologies', *Futures*, March: 115–41.

Ironbridge Gorge Museum, (1989) *Under Fives and Museums: Guidelines for Teachers*, Ironbridge.

Irvine, J. (1990) 'Children of the Future', *Links*, 1: 4–7.

Johnson, D. (1993) 'Academic and Intellectual Foundations of Teacher Education in Global Perspectives', *Theory into Practice*, 32, 1: 3–13.

Johnson, N. (1989) *Teachers and Change: A Literature Review*, Melbourne: Institute of Education, University of Melbourne.

—— (nd) *How do Teachers Learn New Ways of Working? Strategies for Supporting*

School and Teacher Change, Melbourne: Institute of Education, University of Melbourne.

Joicey, H.B. (1986) *An Eye on the Environment: An Art Education Project*, London: Unwin Hyman Ltd. and the World Wide Fund for Nature.

Jones, B.O. (1982) *Sleepers, Wake! Technology and the Future of Work*, Melbourne: Oxford University Press.

—— (1986a) 'Teaching Basic Skills for the Information Age', *Unicorn*, 12, 2: 75–80.

—— (1986b) 'Carnivores, Vegetarians and Beef Consomme', in P. Noyce (ed.) *Futures in Education: The Report*, Melbourne: Commission for the Future and Hawthorn Institute's Centre for Curriculum.

Jose, P.E. (1990) 'Just-World Reasoning in Children's Immanent Justice Judgements', *Child Development*, 61: 1024–33.

Judge, A.J.N. (1993) 'Metaphor and the Language of Futures', *Futures*, April, 1993: 275–88.

Jungk, R. and Jarratt, J. (eds) (1969) *Mankind 2000*, Oslo and London: Universitetsforlaget and Allen and Unwin.

Jungk, R. and Mullert, N. (1987) *Future Workshops: How to Create Desirable Futures*, London: Institute for Social Inventions.

Kaftal, G. (1985) *Iconography of the Saints in the Paintings of North East Italy*, Florence: Sansoni.

Kagan, J. (1989) *Unstable Ideas: Temperament, Cognition and Self*, Cambridge, MA: Harvard University Press.

Kagan, S.L. (1988) 'Current Reforms in Early Childhood Education: Are We Addressing the Issues?', *Young Children*, 43, 2: 27–32.

—— (1991) 'Collaboration in Early Care and Education: What Can and Should We Expect?', *Young Children*, 47, 1: 51–6.

—— (1992) 'Readiness Past, Present, and Future: Shaping the Agenda', *Young Children*, 48, 1: 48–52.

Katz, L. (1984) 'The Young Child in the Year 2000: Setting the Professional Agenda', paper presented at the Minnesota Round Table Meeting in Early Education, Center for Early Education and Development, Minnesota University, Minneapolis (Educational Resources Information Center, ED247011).

—— (1990) 'Impressions of Reggio Emilia Preschools', *Young Children*, 45, 6: 11–12.

—— (1995) *Talks with Teachers of Young Children*, Norwood: Ablex Publishing.

Kauffman, D.L. (1976) *Teaching the Future: A Guide to Future-Oriented Education*, Palm Springs: Etc. Publications.

—— (1980) *Futurism and Future Studies*, Washington, DC: National Education Association.

Kekes, J. (1980) *The Nature of Philosophy*, New Jersey: Rowman and Littlefield.

Keliher, A.V. (1963) 'Believing and Doing', *Childhood Education*, 40, 2: 62–5.

—— (1986) 'Back to Basics or Forward to Fundamentals?', *Young Children*, 41, 6: 42–4.

Kennedy, P. (1993) 'Preparing for the 21st Century: Winners and Losers', *New York Review of Books*, 40, 4: 32–43.

Kessler, S.A. (1991) 'Alternative Perspectives on Early Childhood Education', *Early Childhood Research Quarterly*, 6: 183–97.

Kessler, S.A. and Swadener, B.B. (eds) (1992) *Reconceptualising the Early Childhood Curriculum: Beginning the Dialogue*, New York: Teachers College Press.

Kierstead, F. *et al.* (eds) (1979) *Educational Futures: Sourcebook 1* (Selections from the First Conference of the Education Section), Washington, DC: World Future Society.

Kim, T.C. and Dator, J.A. (ed.) (1994) *Creating a New History for Future Generations*, Future Generations Studies Series 11, Kyoto: Institute for the Integrated Study of Future Generations.

Kinnear, D., Preuss, P. and Rogers, J. (1989) *The Ozone Message: Information and Activities for Teaching about Ozone Depletion and the Greenhouse Effect*, Hawthorn: Australian Conservation Foundation.

Kirschenbaum, H. and Simon, S.B. (1974) 'Values and Futures Movements in Education', in A. Toffler (ed.) *Learning For Tomorrow: The Role of the Future in Education*, New York: Random House.

Kleiber, D.A., Major, W. and Manaster, G. (1993) 'Youths' Outlook on the Future IV: A Third Past–Present Comparison', *Youth & Society*, 24, 4: 349–62.

Klein, J. (1993) 'Wanted: A New Philosophy', *The Unesco Courier*, 8: 12–15.

Knoblauch, C. (1992) 'Australian Adolescents and the Persian Gulf War: Perceptions of the Future', *Youth Studies Australia*, Autumn: 40–6.

Kosky, R., Eshkevari, H.S. and Kneebone, G. (eds) (1992) *Breaking Out: Challenges in Adolescent Mental Health in Australia*, Canberra: Australian Government Printing Service.

Kreidler, W.J. (1984) *Creative Conflict Resolution: More than 200 Activities for Keeping Peace in the Classroom*, Glenview: Scott, Foresman and Company.

Lambert, B. (1994) 'Reasoning and Problem Solving: Contemporary Theoretical Perspectives', paper presented at the Australian Early Childhood Research Conference, Canberra.

Landau, E. (1976) 'The Questions Children Ask', *Futures*, April: 154–62.

Lascarides, V.C. (1992) 'United States Contribution to Children's Rights: An Overview of the 20th Century', *International Journal of Early Childhood*, 24, 2: 41–4.

Lavanchy, S. (1993) 'Environmental Education: How Should We Face it in Early Childhood Education?', *International Journal of Early Childhood*, 25, 1: 37–41.

Leach, P. (1994) *Children First: What our Society Must Do – and is not Doing – for our Children Today*, New York: Alfred A. Knopf.

Lee, C.S. (1992) 'Learning and Understanding Mathematical Symbols: Problems and Research', in M. Horne and M. Supple (eds) *Mathematics: Meeting the Challenge*, Melbourne: Mathematical Association of Victoria.

Lee, S.E. (1980) 'Art against Things', *Australian Journal of Art, II*, 1980: 5–16.

Lee, V.E., Brooks-Gunn, J., Schnur, E. and Liaw, F. (1990) 'Are Head Start Effects Sustained? A Longitudinal Follow-Up Comparison of Disadvantaged Children Attending Head Start, No Preschool, and Other Preschool Programs', *Child Development*, 61, 1: 495–507.

Lees, C. (1989) 'What's the Matter with Teens Today ...?', *The Bulletin*, 19 Dec.: 46–53.

Leitwood, K.A. (1981) 'The Dimensions of Curriculum Innovation', *Journal of Curriculum Studies*, 13, 1: 25–36.

Leonard, G.B. (1968) *Education and Ecstasy*, New York: Dell Publishing Co. Inc.

Lewis, A. and Smith, D. (1993) 'Defining Higher Order Thinking', *Theory into Practice*, 32, 3: 131–7.

Lieberman, A. (1986) 'Collaborative Work', *Educational Leadership*, 43, 5: 4–8.

Lipman, M. (1988) 'Critical Thinking – What Can It Be?', *Educational Leadership*, 46, 1: 38–43.

Livingstone, D.W. (1983) *Class Ideologies and Educational Futures*, Barcombe: The Falmer Press.

Logan, L.M. and Logan, V.G. (1971) *Design for Creative Teaching*, Toronto: McGraw-Hill Company of Canada.

Longfellow Robinson, S. (1985) 'Childhood: Can it be Preserved?', *Childhood Education*, 61, 5: 337–42.

Longstreet, W.S. and Shane, H.G. (1993) *Curriculum for a New Millennium*, Boston: Allyn and Bacon.

Lorenzo, R. (1986) *Some Ideas and Goals for Environmental Education*, Milan: Associazione Italiana World Wildlife Fund, Settore Educazione.

—— (1989) *Let's Shape the Future*, Milan: Associazione Italiana World Wildlife Fund, Settore Educazione.

Lorenzo, R. and Lepore, L. (1988) *Scopriamo l'ambiente urbano: impariamo a conoscere e a migliorare 'le nostre città'*, Rome: Associazione Italiana per il World Wildlife Fund, Quaderni Di Educazione Ambientale, I.

—— (1990) *Immaginiamo il futuro*, Rome: Associazione Italiana World Wildlife Fund, Quaderni Di Educazione Ambientale, II.

Lubeck, S. (1994) 'The Politics of Developmentally Appropriate Practice: Exploring Issues of Culture, Class, and Curriculum', in B.L. Mallory and R.S. New (eds) *Diversity and Developmentally Appropriate Practices: Challenges for Early Childhood Education*, New York: Teachers College Press.

M'Bow, A.M. (1976) 'UNESCO and the World Outlook for Tomorrow', *The Unesco Courier*, March: 24–5.

MacCampbell Buckner, L. (1988) 'On the Fast Track to … ? Is it Early Childhood Education or Early Adulthood Education?', *Young Children*, 43, 5: 5.

Mackenzie, D.A. (1926) *The Migration of Symbols and Their Relations to Beliefs and Customs*, New York: Alfred A. Knopf.

MacDanield, M.A. (1974) 'Tomorrow's Curriculum Today', in A. Toffler (ed.) *Learning for Tomorrow: The Role of the Future in Education*, New York: Random House.

MacGregor, P. (1989) 'Visions of the Future', in R.A. Slaughter (ed.) *Studying the Future: An Introductory Reader*, Melbourne: The Commission for the Future and the Australian Bicentennial Authority.

MacHale, J. (1973) '*Futures Critical: A Review*', in Rome World Special Conference on Futures Research, *Human Futures, Needs, Societies, Technologies*, Guildford: *Futures*, IPC Science and Technology Press Ltd.

Mackay, H. (1981) *Computers, Technology and the Future*, Sydney: Centre for Communication Studies.

MacKillop, S. (1990) *AIC Conference Proceedings No. 13: Preventing Youth Suicide*, proceedings of a conference held 24–26 July 1990, Canberra: Australian Institute of Criminology.

MacKim, M.K. (1993) 'Quality Child Care: What Does it Mean for Individual Infants, Parents and Caregivers?', *Early Childhood Development and Care*, 88: 23–30.

MacKisson, M. (1983) *Chrysalis: Nurturing Creative and Independent Thought in Children, Grades 4–11*, Tuscan: Zephyr Press Learning Materials.

MacLean, S.V. (1992) 'Early Childhood Education and Perceptions of "Curriculum"', *Curriculum Perspectives*, 12, 3: 42–6.

—— (1993) 'What's in a Name? Stakeholder Perceptions on the "Enrichment of the Kindergarten Curriculum"', paper presented at the national conference of the Australian Curriculum Studies Association, Curriculum in Profile: Quality or Inequality, Brisbane, June–July.

McLennan, W. (1996) *Year Book Australia. Number 80*, Australian Bureau of Statistics, ABS Catalogue No. 1301.0, Canberra: Australian Government Publishing Service.

MacNaughton, G. (ed.) (1993a) *Equal Play, Equal Work: An Early Childhood Gender Equity Resource Booklet*, Melbourne: Office of Preschool and Child Care, Health and Community Services with the assistance of the Women's Employment Unit, Department of Business and Employment.

—— (1993b) '"You Can be Dad": Gender and Power in Domestic Discourses and Fantasy Play Within Early Childhood', paper presented to the First Australian Research in Early Childhood Education Conference, Canberra.

MacNaughton, G. and Williams, G. (1998) *Techniques for Teaching Young Children Choices in Theory and Practice*, South Melbourne: Longman.

MacTaggert, R. (1992) 'Confronting "Accountability": Resisting Transnational Corporate Ideology', *Curriculum Perspectives*, 12, 1: 72–8.

Malaguzzi, L. (1994) 'Your Image of the Child: Where Teaching Begins', *Child Care Information Exchange*, 96: 52–61.

—— (1998) 'History, Ideas, and Basic Philosophy: An Interview with Lella Gandini', in C.P. Edwards, L. Gandini and G. Forman (eds)*The Hundred Languages of Children: The Reggio Emilia Approach – Advanced Reflections*, Norwood: Ablex Publishing.

Manning, J. (1990) 'Infants are Powerful Too!', *World Studies Journal*, 8, 1: 34–8.

Marien, M. (1971) 'The Discovery and Fall of the Ignorant Society, 1965–1985', in T. Green (ed.) *Educational Planning in Perspective: Forecasting and Policy Making*, Guildford: *Futures*, IPC Science and Technology Press.

Masini, E.B. (1981) 'Images of the Future by Children', research manuscript, Rome.

—— (1982) 'Reconceptualizing Futures: A Need and a Hope', *World Future Society Bulletin*, Nov.–Dec.: 1–8.

—— (1985) 'Experience of Education towards the Future', *Conference*, 8, 3: 77–85.

—— (1986a) 'Early Education for the 21st Century', *Bernard Van Leer Foundation Newsletter*, May: 7.

—— (1986b) 'Human Development and Childhood', in C.A. Mallman and O. Nudler (eds) *Human Development in its Social Context: A Collective Exploration*, London: Hodder and Stoughton.

—— (1989) 'Women and the Young in Perspective', *Futures*, 21, 1: 60–5.

—— (nd) 'Les Enfants et leurs images du futur', *Temps Libre*, 6: 71–84.

McClure, R.M. (1981) 'The Unfinished Agenda', in L.V. Edinger, P.L. Houts and

D.V. Meyer (eds) *Education in the '80s: Curricula Challenges*, Washington, DC: National Education Association.

Mialarat, G. (1976) *World Survey of Pre-School Children*, Paris: Unesco.

Miles, I. (1993a) 'The Ideologies of Futurists', in J. Fowles (ed.) *Handbook of Futures Research*, Westport, CT: Greenwood Press.

—— (1993b) 'Stranger than Fiction: How Important is Science Fiction for Futures Studies?', *Futures*, April: 1–7.

Ministry of Education (1996) *Te Whāriki he Whārike Mātauranga mō Ngā Mokopuna o Aoteara Early Childhood Curriculum*, Wellington: Learning Media Ltd.

Morris, J. (1991) 'Investing in Children's Learning through the Curriculum', *Early Childhood Development and Care*, 73: 87–93.

Morrison, A. and McIntyre D. (eds) *Social Psychology of Teaching*, Harmondsworth: Penguin Books.

Moskowitz, M. (ed.) (1994) *Thinking about Future Generations*, Future Generations Studies Series 1, Kyoto: Institute for the Integrated Study of Future Generations.

Mumford, L. (1971) *The Pentagon of Power*, London: Secker and Warburg.

—— (1973) 'Technics and the Human Culture', paper presented at Rome World Special Conference on Futures Research, *Human Futures, Needs, Societies, Technologies*, Guildford: *Futures*, IPC Science and Technology Press Ltd.

National Association for the Education of Young Children (1986a) 'Position Statement on Developmentally Appropriate Practice in Early Childhood Programs Serving Children from Birth through Age 8', *Young Children*, 41, 6: 5–19.

—— (1986b) 'Position Statement on Developmentally Appropriate Practice in Programs for 4- and 5-Year-Olds', *Young Children*, 41, 6: 20–9.

—— (1992) 'Guidelines for Appropriate Curriculum Content and Assessment in Programs Serving Children Ages 3 through 8: A Position Statement of the National Association for the Education of Young Children and the National Association of Early Childhood Specialists in State Departments of Education', *Young Children*, March: 21–38.

National Childcare Accreditation Council (1993) *Quality Improvement and Accreditation System Handbook*, Sydney: National Childcare Accreditation Council.

Nestdale, R. (1989) 'Children's Rights for a Better Tomorrow', *Australian Journal of Early Childhood*, 14, 2: 57–9.

Nevitte, N. and Gibbons, R. (1990) *New Elites in Old States: Ideologies in the Anglo-American Democracies*, Toronto: Oxford University Press.

New, R. (1990) 'Excellent Early Education: A City in Italy has it', *Young Children*, 45, 6: 4–10.

Nicholson, S. (1979) 'The Media in the Education of the Child', in S. Doxiadis (ed.) *The Child in the World of Tomorrow: A Window into the Future*, Oxford: Pergamon Press.

Nickerson, R.S. (1992) *Looking Ahead. Human Factors Challenges in a Changing World*, Hillsdale, NJ: Lawrence Erlbaum Associates.

Nowak-Fabrykowski, K. (1994) 'Can Symbolic Play Prepare Children for their Future?', *Early Childhood Development and Care*, 102: 63–9.

Noyce, P. (1986a) 'Ex-Teachers, Ex-Learners and Futures in Education', *In Future*, 3, Nov–Dec: 7–10.

—— (ed.) (1986b) *Futures in Education: The Report*, Melbourne: Commission for the Future and Hawthorn Institute's Centre for Curriculum.

Oboodait, F. (1993) 'To Establish World Peace in Our Planet, We Should Vision the Inter-Planetary Peace for Our Children', *International Journal of Early Childhood*, 25, 1: 33–6.

Ochiltree, G. (1994) *Effects of Child Care on Young Children: Forty Years of Research*, Early Childhood Study Paper No. 5, Melbourne: Australian Institute of Family Studies.

Ochiltree, G. and Edgar, D. (1995) *Today's Child Care, Tomorrow's Children!* Early Childhood Study Paper No. 7, Melbourne: Australian Institute of Family Studies.

Oliver, S. (1991–2)'Speaking Futuristically, Optimistically', *21.C*, 4, Summer: 38.

Olson, J.K. (1980) 'Teacher Constructs and Curriculum Change', *Journal of Curriculum Studies*, 12, 1: 1–11.

Orsini-Romano, C. and Pascale, I.D. (1978) *Planning Tomorrow's Curriculum Today*, Washington, DC: US Department of Education, National Institute of Education (Educational Resources Information Center, ED169040).

Osborn, A.F. and Milbank, J.E. (1993) *The Effects of Early Education: A Report from the Child Health and Education Study*, New York: Oxford University Press.

Page, J. (1991) 'Critical Futures Studies: Rendering the Early Childhood Curriculum Responsive to the Future Needs of Children', *Australian Journal of Early Childhood*, 16, 4: 43–8.

—— (1992) 'Symbolising the Future: Developing a Futures Iconography', *Futures*, December: 1056–63.

—— (1993) 'Advocating the Future Rights of Our Children', *Journal of Australian Early Childhood Association*, 11, 3: 35–41.

—— (1994a) 'Curriculum Priorities for the Next Century: Futures Studies and the National Curriculum', *Australian Journal of Early Childhood*, 19, 1: 34–9. Republished as J. Page (1994b) 'Futures Studies and the Early Childhood Curriculum', in G. Halliwell (ed.) *Early Childhood Perspectives on Assessment, Justice and Quality, Living and Learning Together: A Selection of Papers From the ACSA Curriculum '93 Conference*, Canberra: Australian Curriculum Studies Association.

—— (1996) 'Education Systems as Agents of Change: An Overview of Futures Education', in R.A. Slaughter (ed.) *New Thinking for a New Millennium*, London: Routledge.

—— (1998a) 'Futures in Early Childhood Education', in D. Hicks and R.A. Slaughter (eds) *World Yearbook of Education 1998: Futures Education*, London: Kogan Page.

—— (1998b) 'The Four- and Five-Year-Old's Understanding of the Future: A Preliminary Study, *Futures*, 30, 9: 913–22.

Panofsky, E. (1939) *Studies in Iconography: Humanistic Themes in the Art of the Renaissance*, New York: Oxford University Press.

Park, D. (1978) 'The Past and the Future', in J.T. Fraser, N. Lawrence and D. Park (eds)*The Study of Time III*, Berlin: Springer-Verlag.

Parliamentary Office of Science and Technology, (1993) 'Screen Violence', *The Psychologist*, August: 353–6.

Parry, A. (1993) 'Children Surviving in a Violent World – "Choosing Non-Violence"', *Young Children*, 48, 6: 13–84.

Patterson, C.J. (1992) 'Essential Curriculum Decision-Making for Children Under Three Years of Age', *Curriculum Perspectives*, 12, 3: 50–3.

Patterson, C.J., Kupersmidt, J.B. and Griesler, P.C. (1990) "Children's Perceptions of Self and of Relationships with Others as a Function of Sociometric Status', *Child Development*, 61: 1335–49.

Payne, M. (1989) 'Under Fives at the Tate', *Nursery World*, September: 12–14.

—— (1993) 'Games Children Play: Playthings as User Friendly Aids for Learning in Art Appreciation', *Early Childhood Development and Care*, 89: 101–16.

Pelizzoli, L., Lombardini, M.C. and Martino, A.D. (1977) 'Images from School: The Views of Italian Teachers and Pupils', *Futures*, 1977: 160–6.

Perelman, L.J. (1988) 'Restructuring the System is the Solution', *Phi Delta Kappan*, 70, 1: 20–4.

Perry, R. (1981) 'Current Curriculum Ideas and Practices in Queensland', *Australian Association of Early Childhood Educators, Bulletin*, 15: 28–33.

—— (1992) 'Experiences Sharing Views about Curriculum', *Curriculum Perspectives*, 12, 3: 46–50.

Pesanelli, D. (1991) 'Reinventing the Children's Room', *The Futurist*, Sept.–Oct.: 28–32.

Peters, D.L. and Klein, E.L. (1981) 'The Education of Young Children: Perspectives on Possible Futures', *Theory into Practice*, 20, 2: 141–7.

Philipsen, M. and Agnew, J. (1996) 'Heart, Mind and Soul: Head Start as a Reminder of the Powerful Function of Schools for their Communities', in J.A. Hatch (ed.) *Qualitative Research in Early Childhood Settings*, Westport, CT: Praeger.

Phillips, C.B. (1988) 'Nurturing Diversity for Today's Children and Tomorrow's Leaders', *Young Children*, 43, 2: 42–7.

Piaget, J. (1951) *Play, Dreams and Imitation in Childhood*, London: Routledge and Kegan Paul.

—— (1953) *The Origin of Intelligence in the Child*, London: Routledge and Kegan Paul.

—— (1955) *The Child's Construction of Reality*, London: Routledge and Kegan Paul.

Pierce, C.M. (1980) 'The Pre-Schooler and the Future', in L. Jennings and S. Cornish (eds) *Education and the Future*, Bethesda: World Future Society.

Pike, G. and Selby, D. (1988) *Global Teacher, Global Learner*, London: Hodder and Stoughton in association with the Centre for Global Education, University of York.

Piscitelli, B. (1991) 'Children in Museums', in S. Wright (ed.) *The Arts in Early Childhood*, New York: Prentice Hall.

Polak, F. (1961) *The Image of the Future*, trans. E. Boulding, New York: Oceana Press.

Postman, N. (1987) 'Intellectual Deviants in the Technological Era', keynote address at the Second International Congress on Early Childhood Education, Childhood in the Technological Era, Tel Aviv, 6 July.

Postman, N. and Weingartner, C. (1969) *Teaching as a Subversive Activity*, New York: Dell Publishing Co.

—— (1970) 'Making Contact: Towards the Relevant Curriculum', in R. Gross and B. Gross (eds) *What's Worth Knowing in Radical School Reform*, New York: Simon and Schuster.

Poussaint, A.F. (1974) 'The Black Child's Image of the Future', in A. Toffler (ed.) *Learning For Tomorrow: The Role of the Future in Education*, New York: Random House.

Powell, D.R. (1991) 'Parents and Programmes: Early Childhood as a Pioneer in Parent Involvement and Support', in S.L. Kagan (ed.) *The Care and Education of America's Young Children: Obstacles and Opportunities*, Nineteenth Yearbook of the National Society for the Study of Education, Part 1, Chicago: University of Chicago Press.

Power, M.B. (1993) 'Early Childhood Education: Everyone's Challenge for the 21st Century', *Early Childhood Development and Care*, 86: 53–9.

Pulliam, J.D. (1980) 'Toward a Futuristic Theory of Education', paper presented at the Global Conference on the Future, Toronto (Educational Resources Information Center, ED189010).

Pulliam, J.D. and Bowman, J.R. (1974) *Educational Futurism: In Pursuance of Survival*, Oklahoma: University of Oklahoma Press.

Rabin, A.I. (1978) 'Future Time Perspective and Ego Strength', in J.T. Fraser, N. Lawrence and D. Park (eds) *The Study of Time III*, Berlin: Springer-Verlag.

Ravitch, D. (1983) 'On Thinking about the Future', *Phi Delta Kappan*, 64, 5: 317–20.

Raviv, A., Oppenheimer, L. and Bar-Tal, D. (eds) (1999) *How Children Understand War and Peace: A Call for International Peace Education*, San Francisco: Jossey-Bass Publishers.

Ray, D. *et al.* (1994) *Education for Human Rights: An International Perspective*, Paris: Unesco, International Bureau of Education.

Raynor, N.O. and Entin, E.E. (1993) 'The Function of Future Orientation as a Determinant of Human Behaviour in Step-Path Theory of Action', *International Journal of Psychology*, 18: 463–87.

Reardon, B.A. (1997a) *Tolerance – The Threshold of Peace*, Unit 1: Teacher training resource unit, Paris: Unesco.

—— (1997b) *Tolerance – The Threshold of Peace*, Unit 2: Primary school resource unit, Paris: Unesco.

—— (1997c) *Tolerance – The Threshold of Peace*, Unit 3: Secondary school resource unit, Paris: Unesco.

Richmond, G. (1989) 'The Future School: Is Lowell Pointing us Toward a Revolution in Education?', *Phi Delta Kappan*, 71, 3: 232–6.

Ritchie, J. (1996) 'The Bicultural Imperative within the New Zealand Draft Curriculum Guidelines for Early Childhood Education, "Te Whariki"', *Australian Journal of Early Childhood*, 21, 3: 28–32.

Rodd, J. (1998) *Leadership in Early Childhood: The Pathway to Professionalism*, St Leonards: Allen and Unwin.

Rogers, M. and Tough, A. (1992) 'What Happens When Students Face the Future?', *Futures Research Quarterly*, 8, 4: 9–18.

Rome World Special Conference on Futures Research (1974) *Human Futures, Needs, Societies, Technologies*, Guildford: *Futures*, IPC Science and Technology Press.

Roper, D.L. (1989) *A Study in Foresight*, Truro: Cedar Books.

Roskos, K. (1990) 'A Taxonomic View of Pretend Play Activity among 4- and 5-Year-Old Children', *Early Childhood Research Quarterly*, 5, 1: 495–512.

Ross, A. (1991) *Strange Weather: Culture, Science and Technology in the Age of Limits*, London: Verso.

Rubinsky, Y. and Wiseman, I. (1982) *The History of the End of the World*, New York: Quill.

Ryan, S. (1986) 'Education Launched', *In Future*, 3, Nov.–Dec.: 11.

Sachs, C. (1990) *Exploring the Human Dimensions of Development: A Review of the Literature*, Paris: Unesco, Bureau of Studies and Programming Major Programme 1, Reflection on World Problems and Future-Oriented Studies, Studies and Documents.

Salner, M. (1986) 'Adult Cognitive and Epistemological Development in Systems Education', *Systems Research*, 3, 4: 225–32.

Saracho, O.N. and Spodek, B. (1993) 'Professionalism and the Preparation of Early Childhood Education Practitioners', *Early Childhood Development and Care*, 89: 1–17.

Saunders, S.A. and Green, V. (1993) 'Evaluating the Social Competence of Young Children: A Review of the Literature', *Early Child Development and Care*, 87: 39–46.

Scheckley, R. (1978) *Futureopolis: Impossible Cities of Science Fiction and Fantasy*, New York: Bergstrom and Boyle Books Ltd.

Schmidt, F. and Friedman, A. (1985) *Creative Conflict Solving for Kids Grades 4–9*, Miami: Grace Contrino Abrams Peace Education Foundation Inc.

Schön, D.S. (1992) 'The Theory of Inquiry: Dewey's Legacy to Education', *Curriculum Inquiry*, 22, 2: 119–39.

Schwartz, P. *et al.* (1977) 'In Search of Tomorrow's Crises', *The Futurist*, October: 269–78.

Schwarz, S. (ed.) (1976) *Knowledge and Concepts in Futures Studies*, Boulder, CO: Westview Press Inc.

Schweinhart, L.J., Barnes, H.V. and Weikart, D.P. (1993) *Significant Benefits: The High/Scope Perry Preschool Study through Age 27*, Monograph 10, Ypsilanti: The High/Scope Educational Research Foundation.

Scorer, R. (1988) 'The Council for Posterity', *Journal of the Institute for Social Inventions*, 13: 1–4.

Scott, C. (1998) 'An Exploration of the Development of Young Children's Understanding of Time Concepts', *Australian Journal of Early Childhood*, 23, 2: 6–12.

Scutt, J. (1992) 'Practice and Professionalism in Early Childhood: A Positive Ethos for Early Childhood', in B. Lambert (ed.) *Changing Faces: The Early Childhood Profession in Australia*, Watson: Australian Early Childhood Association.

Seif, E. (1979) *Dare We Build a New Curriculum for a New Age?*, Washington, DC: US Department of Education, National Institute of Education (Educational Resources Information Center, ED184937).

Shane, H.G. (1975) 'Social Decisions and Educational Policy', in L. Rubin, *The Future of Education: Perspectives on Tomorrow's Schooling*, Boston: Allyn and Bacon.

—— (1977) *Curriculum Change toward the 21st Century*, Washington, DC: National Education Association, Curriculum Series.

—— (1982) 'The Silicon Age and Education', *Phi Delta Kappan*, 63, 5: 303–8.

Shane, H.G. and Shane, J.G. (1974) 'Educating the Youngest for Tomorrow', in A. Toffler (ed.) *Learning for Tomorrow: The Role of the Future in Education*, New York: Random House.

Shane, H.G. and Tabler, M.B. (1981) *Educating for a New Millennium: Views of 132 International Scholars*, Bloomington: Phi Delta Kappan Educational Foundation.

Shanker, A. (1986) 'Teachers Must Take Charge', *Educational Leadership*, 44, 1: 12–13.

Sharpe, C. (1999) 'Systems Advocacy in a Changing Political Climate', *Rattler*, 49, Spring: 5–7.

Shoji, M. (1992) 'The Defences of Peace Must Be Constructed in the Minds of Young Children', in E.H. Ishigaki (ed.) *Asian Young Children: Report of OMEP Asian Seminar 1989*, Tokyo: Kazama-Shobo.

Short, V.M. (1991) 'Childhood Education in a Changing World', *Childhood Education*, 68, 1: 10–13.

Sigel, I.E. (1987) 'Does Hothousing Rob Children of their Childhood?', *Early Childhood Research Quarterly*, 2, 3: 221–5.

Sigelman, C.K. and Waitzman, K.A. (1991) 'The Development of Distributive Justice Orientations: Contextual Influences on Children's Resource Allocations', *Child Development*, 62: 1367–78.

Silin, J.G. (1988) 'On Becoming Knowledgeable Professionals', in O.N. Saracho and D.L. Peters (eds) *Professionalism and the Early Childhood Practitioner*, New York: Teachers College Press.

—— (1995) *Sex, Death, and the Education of Children: Our Passion for Ignorance in the Age of AIDS*, New York: Teachers College Press.

Silver, P.F. and Moyle, C.R.J. (1985) 'The Impact of School Leadership on School Effectiveness', *Educator's Magazine*, 42, 2: 42–5.

Singer, B.D. (1974) 'The Future-Focused Role Image', in A. Toffler (ed.) *Learning for Tomorrow: The Role of the Future in Education*, New York: Random House.

Siraj-Blatchford, J. (1995) 'Racial Equality Education: Identity Curriculum and Pedagogy', in J. Siraj-Blatchford (eds) *Educating the Whole Child. Cross Curricular Skills, Themes and Dimensions*, Buckingham: Open University Press.

Siraj-Blatchford, J. and Patel, L. (1995) 'Understanding Environmental Education for the Primary Classroom', in J. Siraj-Blatchford and I. Siraj-Blatchford (eds) *Educating the Whole Child: Cross-Curricular Skills, Themes and Dimensions*, Buckingham: Open University Press.

Siraj-Blatchford, J. and Siraj-Blatchford, L. (1995) 'Cross-Curricular Skills, Themes and Dimensions: An Introduction', in J. Siraj-Blatchford and I. Siraj-Blatchford (eds) *Educating the Whole Child: Cross-Curricular Skills, Themes and Dimensions*, Buckingham: Open University Press.

Skeggs, B. (1997) *Formations of Class and Gender*, London: Sage Publications.

Skertchly, A.R.B. (1980) 'Education and Technological Change', *Unicorn*, 6, 1: 6–17.

Slaughter, R.A. (1985) *What Do We Do Now the Future is Here? Essays on Futures, Education and the Speculative Imagination*, Lancaster: University of Lancaster, Department of Educational Research.

—— (1986) *Futures Across the Curriculum: A Handbook of Tools and Techniques*, Lancaster: University of Lancaster, Department of Educational Research.

—— (1988) *Recovering the Future*, Clayton: Graduate School of Environmental Science, Monash University.

—— (1989a) 'Cultural Reconstruction in the Post-Modern World', *Journal of Curriculum Studies*, 21, 3: 255–70.

—— (1989b) 'Probing Beneath the Surface: Review of a Decade's Futures Work', *Futures*, October: 452–64.

—— (ed.) (1989c) *Studying the Future: An Introductory Reader*, Melbourne: Commission for the Future and the Australian Bicentennial Authority of Victoria.

—— (1990a) *Aspects of Critical Futures Study*, Melbourne: Institute of Education, University of Melbourne.

—— (1990b) *The Foresight Principle*, Melbourne: Institute of Education, University of Melbourne.

—— (1990c) '*A Personal Annotated Bibliography of the Future*', Melbourne: Institute of Education, University of Melbourne.

—— (1991a) 'Changing Images of Futures in the 20th Century', *Futures*, June: 499–515.

—— (1991b) *Futures Concepts and Powerful Ideas*, Melbourne: Futures Study Centre.

—— (1991c) 'An International Overview of Futures Education', report for Unesco's Clearinghouse for the Future, Melbourne.

—— (1993a) 'The Substantive Knowledge Base of Futures Studies', *Futures*, April: 227–33.

—— (1993b) 'Futures Concepts', *Futures*, April: 289–314.

—— (1994) *From Fatalism to Foresight, Educating for the Early 21st Century: A Framework for Considering Young People's Needs Over the Next 20 Years*, Hawthorn: Australian Council for Educational Administration.

—— (1997a) 'A Foresight Strategy for Future Generations', *Futures*, 29, 8: 723–30.

—— (1997b) 'Developing and Applying Strategic Foresight', *The ABN Report on Learning, Leadership and the Future*, 5, 10: 7–15

—— (1998) 'Futures beyond Dystopia', *Futures*, 30, 10: 993–1002.

Slavin, R.E. (1987) 'Developmental and Motivational Perspectives on Cooperative Learning: A Reconciliation', *Child Development*, 58: 1161–7.

Smart, J. (ed.) (1991) *My World: Exploring the Future*, Godalming: Scholastic Publications Ltd. on behalf of the World Wide Fund for Nature.

Smetana, J.G., Schlagman, N. and Adams, P. (1993) 'Preschool Children's Judgements about Hypothetical and Actual Transgressions', *Child Development*, 64, 1: 202–14.

Smith, D.L. and Lovat, T.J. (1991) *Curriculum: Action on Reflection*, Wentworth Falls, NSW: Social Science Press.

Smith, V.H. (1973) 'Old Taboos: New Realities', *Educational Leadership*, 31, 1: 6–9.

Smyth, J. (ed.) (1998) *World Education Report 1998: Teachers and Teaching in a Changing World*, Paris: Unesco.

Speight, G. (1987) *People, Culture and Change, Controlling Our Future*, Wentworth Falls: Social Science Press.

Spodek, B. (1970) 'What are the Sources of Early Childhood Curriculum?', *Young Children*, 26, 1: 48–58.

Spodek, B. and Brown, P.C. 'Curriculum Alternatives in Early Childhood Education: A Historical Perspective', in B. Spodek (ed.) *Handbook of Research on the Education of Young Children*, New York: Macmillan.

Spradley, J.P. (1980) *Participant Observation*, New York: Holt, Rinehart and Winston.

Sroufe, L., Egeland, B. and Kreutzer, T. (1990) 'The Fate of Early Experience Following Developmental Change: Longitudinal Approaches to Individual Adaptation in Childhood', *Child Development*, 61, 1: 1363–73.

Stiles, J., Delis, D. and Tada, W. (1991) 'Global–Local Processing in Preschool Children', *Child Development*, 62: 1258–75.

Stonehouse, A. (1992) 'Care and Education – What's the Difference?', *Curriculum Perspectives*, 12, 3: 53–6.

Sundgren, L. (ed.) (1983) *Education for International Co-operation and Peace at the Primary-School Level*, Paris: Unesco.

Sungaila, H. (1983) 'The New Technology: Danger or Deliverance for Australian Education?', *Unicorn*, 9, 1: 28–33.

Svetka, S. (1996) 'Head Start and Early Head Start Programs: What We Have Learned Over the Last 30 Years about Preschool, Families and Communities?', *International Journal of Early Childhood*, 26, 1: 59–62.

Takanishi, R. (1981) 'Early Childhood Education and Research: The Changing Relationship', *Theory into Practice*, 20, 2: 86–92.

Taylor, M., Cartwright, B. and Bowden, T. (1991) 'Perspective-Taking and Theory of Mind: Do Children Predict Interpretative Diversity as a Function of Differences in Observers' Knowledge?', *Child Development*, 62, 6: 1334–51.

Teahan, J.E. (1958) 'Future Time Perspective, Optimism, and Academic Achievement', *Journal of Abnormal and Social Psychology*, 57: 379–80.

Tepperman, L. and Curtis, J. (1995) 'Popular Images of the Future: Cross-National Survey Results, 1981 and 1991', *Futures*, 27, 5: 549–70.

Thompson, A.E. (1979) *Understanding Futurology: An Introduction to Futures Study*, Newton Abbot: David and Charles.

Thorkildsen, T.A. (1989) 'Pluralism in Children's Reasoning about Social Justice', *Child Development*, 60: 965–72.

Tickell, G. (1987) 'Developing Curriculum Materials for the Future', *In Future*, 5, April–May: 17–19.

—— (1989) 'The BFEP Experience', in R.A. Slaughter (ed.) *Studying the Future: An Introductory Reader*, Melbourne: Commission for the Future and the Australian Bicentennial Authority of Victoria.

Tickell, G. and Peterson, C. (1987) 'Futures Education Project Report', *In Future*, 7, Dec.: 14.

Tinkler, D.E. (1987) 'Change and Choices for Education: Learning and Teaching for the Future', paper presented at the Australian Education Conference, Wesley College, Perth, 29 Sept.

Tinworth, S. (1997) 'Whose Good Idea was It? Child-Initiated Curriculum', *Australian Journal of Early Childhood*, 22, 3: 24–8.

Toda, M. (1993) 'Future Time Perspective and Human Cognition: An Evolutional View', *International Journal of Psychology*, 18: 351–64.

Toffler, A. (1970) *Future Shock*, London: The Bodley Head.

—— (ed.) (1972) *The Futurists*, New York: Random House.

—— (1973) 'Learning to Live with Future Shock', in R.W. Holstrop (ed.) *Foundations of Futurology in Education*, Homewood: Etc. Publications.

—— (1974) 'The Psychology of the Future', in A. Toffler (ed.) *Learning for Tomorrow: The Role of the Future in Education*, New York: Random House.

—— (1980) *The Third Wave*, London: Pan Books.

Tough, A. (1991) *Crucial Questions about the Future*, Lanham, MD: Lanham University Press of America.

Trommsdorff, G. (1993) 'Future Orientation and Socialisation', *International Journal of Psychology*, 18: 381–406.

Trommsdorff, G. and Lamm, H. (1975) 'An Analysis of Future Orientation and Some of its Social Determinants', in J.T. Fraser and N. Lawrence (eds) *The Study of Time II*, Berlin: Springer-Verlag.

Troutman, B.I. and Palombo, R.D. (1983) 'Identifying Futures Trends in Curriculum Planning', *Educational Leadership*, 41, 1: 49.

Tydeman, J. (1987) *Futures Methodologies Handbook: An Overview of Futures Research Methodologies and Techniques*, Melbourne: Commission for the Future.

Unesco (1987) *The World by the Year 2000*, Paris: Unesco.

—— (1991) *World Education Report 1991*, Paris : Unesco.

—— (1995) *World Education Report 1995*, Paris : Unesco.

Unicef (1990a) *The World Summit for Children*, New York: Unicef.

—— (1990b) *World Summit for Children: Words and Images*, New York: Unicef.

—— (1991) *The State of the World's Children 1991*, Oxford: Oxford University Press.

—— (1995) *The State of the World's Children 1995*, Oxford: Oxford University Press.

—— (1996) *The State of the World's Children 1996*, Oxford: Oxford University Press.

—— (1997) *The State of the World's Children 1997*, Oxford: Oxford University Press.

—— (1998)*The State of the World's Children 1998*, Oxford: Oxford University Press.

Vaizey, J. (1962) *Education for Tomorrow*, Harmondsworth: Penguin Books.

Vale, C. and Roughead, C. (1987) 'Whose Culture Does Education Transmit? Exclusive Curriculum as a Source of Inequality', *Curriculum Perspectives*, 7, 1: 58–61.

Van Avery, D. (1980) 'Futuristics and Education', *Educational Leadership*, 37, 5: 441–2.

Van Avery, D., Fletcher, G., Glines, D., Roth, V. and Stock, R. (1979) *Futuristics and Education: An ASCD Task Force Report*, Alexandria: Association for Supervision and Curriculum Development.

Van der Eyken, W. (1967) *The Pre-School Years*, Harmondsworth: Penguin Books.

Van Scoy, I.J. and Fairchild, S.H. (1993) 'It's about Time! Helping Preschool and Primary Children Understand Time Concepts', *Young Child*, 48, 2: 21–4.

Vygotsky, L.S. (1978) *Mind in Society: The Development of Higher Psychological Processes*, edited by M. Cole, Cambridge, MA: Harvard University Press.

Wagschal, P.M. and Johnson, L. (1986) 'Children's Views of the Future: Innocence Almost Lost', *Phi Delta Kappan*, 67, 9: 666–9.

Wallis, C.N. (1979) 'Future-Oriented Preschool Education', PhD dissertation, University of Tennessee, Knoxville.

Wasik, B.H., Ramey, C.T., Bryant, D.M. and Sparling, J.J. (1990) 'A Longitudinal Study of Two Early Intervention Strategies: Project CARE', *Child Development*, 61, 1: 1682–96.

Waters, J. (1998) *Helping Young Children Understand their Rights*, Carlton, VIC: National Secretariat World Organisation for Early Childhood Education (OMEP).

Watkins, P.E. (1980) 'Education, Technology and Deskilling', *Unicorn*, 6, 1: 18–24.

—— (1986) 'Forecasting the Technological Future: Directions for Education', *Unicorn*, 12, 2: 81–6.

Watt, J. (1988) *Evaluation in Action: A Case Study of an Under-Fives Centre in Scotland*, The Hague: Bernard Van Leer Foundation, Occasional Paper 3.

Watts, B. (1987) 'Changing Families – Changing Children's Services: Where are the Children Going? Are Kindergarten Teachers Ready to Go Too?', *Australian Journal of Early Childhood*, 12, 3: 4–12.

Weikart, D.P. (1989) 'Hard Choices in Early Childhood Care and Education: A View to the Future', *Young Children*, 44, 3: 25–30.

Weikart, D.P., Bond, J.T. and McNeil, J.T. (1978) *The Ypsilanti Perry Preschool Project: Preschool Years and Longitudinal Results through Fourth Grade*, Monographs of the High/Scope Educational Research Foundation No. 3, Ypsilanti: High/Scope Educational Research Foundation.

Wemmeyer, L.B. (1986) *Futuristics*, New York: Franklin Watts.

Wentzel, K.R. (1991) 'Relations between Social Competence and Academic Achievement in Early Adolescence', *Child Development*, 62: 1066–77.

Whaley, C.E. (1984) *Futures Studies: Personal and Global Possibilities*, New York: Trillium Press.

Whitrow, G.J. (1980) *The Natural Philosophy of Time*, Oxford: Clarendon Press.

Wilber, K. (1983) *Eye to Eye: The Quest for a New Paradigm*, Boston, MA: Shambala.

Williams, L.R. and Fromberg D.P. (eds) (1992) *Encyclopaedia of Early Childhood Education*, New York: Garland Publishing.

Wilson, B. and Wyn, J. (1987) *Shaping Futures: Youth Action for Livelihood*, Sydney: Allen and Unwin.

—— (1990) 'Social Outcomes, Power and Education', *Curriculum Perspectives*, 10, 2: 1–9.

—— (1985) *Young People's Views of Our World: The Implications for Peace Education*, Melbourne: Victorian Association for Peace Studies.

Wilson, N. (1989) 'The State of the Planet and Young Children's Minds', in R.A. Slaughter (ed.) *Studying the Future: An Introductory Reader*, Melbourne: The Commission for the Future and the Australian Bicentennial Authority.

Wilson, T.W. Jr (1985) 'The Global Environment and the Quest for Peace: A Revolution in the Scale of Things', *Social Education*, March: 201–4.

Windham, D.M. (ed.) (1992) *Education for All: The Requirements*, Roundtable Themes 111, World Conference on Education for All, at Jomtein, Thailand, Paris: Unesco.

Winthrop, H. (1971) 'Utopia Construction and Future Forecasting: Problems, Limitations, and Relevance', in W. Bell and J.A. Mau (eds) *The Sociology of the Future*, New York: Russell Sage Foundation.

Wittock, A. (1960) *Symbols Signs and their Meaning*, London: Leonard Hill Books Ltd.

Woodhead, M. (1985) 'Pre-School Education has Long-Term Effects: But can They be Generalised?' *Oxford Review of Education*, 11, 2: 133–55.

Woodhead, M. *et al.* (1991) *Growing up in a Changing Society*, Child Development in Social Context 3, London: Routledge.

Wolf, A.D. (1990) 'Art Postcards – Another Aspect of Your Aesthetics Program?', *Young Children*, January: 39–43.

Yates, L. (1987) 'Inclusive Curriculum', *Curriculum Perspectives*, 7, 1: 57–8.

Younan, S. (1993) 'The Devalued Image', *The Unesco Courier*, 11, July–Aug.: 21–6.

Zigler, E. and Muenchow, S. (1992) *Head Start: The Inside Story of America's Most Successful Educational Experiment*, New York: Basic Books.

Zigler, E. and Styfco, S.J. (eds) (1993) *Head Start and Beyond: A National Plan for Extended Childhood Intervention*, New Haven, CT: Yale University Press.

Index